NE\

PM Story Books
TEACHERS' GUIDE
Green Level

ANNETTE SMITH

RUTLAND ELEMENTARY SCHOOL

NELSON PRICE MILBURN

Acknowledgements

The author and publisher would like to thank the following copyright
holders for permission to reproduce these poems.

'Candlelight' from *Junior poetry* by A.C. Lundon.
Published by Curriculum Concepts (NZ) Ltd, 1993.
Reprinted by permission of the publisher.

'Wanted' by Rose Fyleman.
Permission granted by The Society of Authors as the literary
representative of the Estate of Rose Fyleman.

First published in New Zealand in 1996 by
Nelson Price Milburn
1 Te Puni Street, Petone
WELLINGTON

© Annette Smith 1996

10 9 8 7 6 5 4
05 04 03 02 01 00

PM Story Books Teachers' Guide: Green Level

ISBN 1 86955 636 4

Cover and design by Josie Semmler
Photographs by Margi Moore
Paged by J&M Typesetting Services
Illustrated by Boris Silvestri
Printed in Australia by Australian Print Group

Contents

About the *New PM Story Books*

The basic philosophy

'Children learn best with books that have meaning and are rewarding' ... *Reading in Junior Classes*, New Zealand Department of Education.

'I can read this!' The revised *New PM Story Books*, centred on meaning, are also designed to give children the rewarding experience of success. If a child can read one book they should be able to read another and another. Success should follow success. When the right match of 'child to book' is made, the greater the interest and the greater the youngster's motivation to read.

Twenty-five years of testing in schools

The original PM Methuen Story Books were published between 1963 and 1976. They were written to support the first twelve books in the New Zealand Department of Education's Ready to Read series (1963) and were used extensively — and old copies are still being used — in New Zealand, Australia, Canada, Britain and the USA.

The quality of these books has made them endure. The series was an unusual one for its time — the simple but widely varied stories, told with very few words, held the interest of young children. (Will hungry Tiger catch Baby Monkey? Will Bill find his Teddy?) The best books had properly shaped plots with tension, a climax and a satisfying ending. Children enjoyed early successful experiences with print, because of this story quality — and because new basic vocabulary was introduced slowly.

Care was taken, too, with the sentence structures, the choice of clear well-spaced type, and with the meaningful accurate illustrations. Because the books were easy as

well as interesting, children were able to practise a variety of reading skills and enjoy the feedback of success. They learned new words — and practised them again and again — all the time understanding what they were reading about, and returning to the stories with pleasure *because* they were stories with real meaning.

The criticism levelled at many 'stories' written for beginners is that most are not stories — they are repetitious reading exercises in which meaning comes a poor second. Teachers and children have often been disappointed by the bland banality of most early school 'readers', with pages that were shaped not by a story-teller but by a need to repeat known words, or letter clusters, as often as possible. In revulsion from these interest-starved, over-repetitive non-literary exercises, many modern teachers have built their reading programmes around library picture books that are worth reading for their own sake — only to discover that too many children are defeated when presented with 200 or so basic words in quick succession. It is not easy for average beginners to sort out *we were was with will wet who why what when where which went want won't walk work wash warm word* ... It never will be!

The authors of the original PM books worked hard to combine the virtues of both approaches — controlled basic vocabulary to let children master a growing number of common but confusing basic words, *and* story-telling quality to engage the mind and emotions and make learning to read satisfying.

In the 1980s many New Zealand teachers repeatedly asked if their favourite PM Methuen Story Books could be reprinted. Because of these requests Beverley Randell (author of most of the original books) and a team of experienced practising teachers have together updated the best of the stories and added a dozen exciting new titles. (Will Tyrannosaurus eat Triceratops? Will Mother Penguin dodge the hungry seal?) The story quality for which the books were loved has been kept and strengthened in the revised series, but not at the expense of simplicity – the books are still easy to read.

Features of the New PM Story Books

The revised books have many ingredients, and all stories, old and new, were rigorously considered and shaped to meet the criteria: **all stories have**

- *meaningful content*. The situations and concepts can be understood by young children. The resolution in each story is logical — these stories encourage children to think by *letting* them think. The books are full of opportunities for intelligent discussion and logical prediction.
- *well shaped plots*. Tension appears early in each story — something goes amiss — and the problem is solved by the end. It is tension that keeps children and teachers interested in the story — what will happen next? When the problem is finally resolved the ending is satisfying.
- *no sexism, racism or stereotyping of people*. As before, Sally is resourceful, Ben helps make a cake, Jessica likes climbing trees, Tom is brave (but is allowed to cry). Now Gran rides the farm bike … some Dads are mechanically minded, and some are not … Sally's Mum, a single parent, goes to work …
- *a wide spread of subjects* to meet the different experiences and enthusiasms of as many children as possible. There are stories about everyday life at home and out of doors, the crises of fire and flood, busy bulldozers and helicopters, familiar farm and garden animals and pets. Danger faced by animals in the wild is a recurring theme. The popular stories about the Bear family bring in fantasy, and there are some retold fables, a new interest is sport (Will Tim win the race? Will he get to football on time?).
- *characters that are satisfyingly true to themselves* — for example the books about Ben and his Mum show a consistent love of books, Tim is keen on sport, Sally is resourceful, Jessica is the responsible elder child, and so on.
- *language that is natural*. These books are easy to read because they contain the familiar constructions children expect.
- *language that is satisfying to the ear*. The rhythms of good English, story-teller's English, are there.
- *considerable scientific accuracy*. Twenty or so stories about animals (appealing subjects in their own right) lead to greater understanding of the environment. Several stories about common or garden animals (hedgehog, lizard, seagull, spider, snail) encourage young children to observe for themselves.
- *attractive well-drawn illustrations* that enable children to gain maximum understanding as they match picture with text, and vice versa. Meticulous care has been taken with these hardworking pictures. There are books that children will return to again and again with delight. When they compare one book with another about the same children, they will find that details match in a satisfying way.

- *warmth and emotional sensitivity*. The child heroes are successful problem solvers — they are never laughed at, never made to look inadequate.
- *individually designed glossy covers*, decorated title pages, numbered pages and a larger format than in the first edition, which was published at a time when 'school readers' looked like school readers. Now they look like picture books.
- *unobtrusive grading*. A 'daisy petal clock' with twelve outlined petals appears on each back cover. On each clock one or two petals are fully coloured, showing teachers the approximate level for each book. Few children will notice this 'hand' on the daisy clock. It looks like a publisher's logo, rather than a grading device.
- *names that will sound familiar* to children in the 1990s. Bill has become Ben, Kate has replaced Ann, Martin has become James, and Jean is now Jessica. Mother and Father are now Mum and Dad (Mother Bear, Mother Monkey, Mother Sheep are still there).
- *more elisions*. It's and let's, found in the original series, have been joined by I'm, he's, can't, don't, won't and that's. Elisions make conversations sound less stilted and more natural.
- *a rate of new word introduction held*, after the Red Level, to *1:20* (*no more than one new word in every 20 running words*). When difficulties do not appear too frequently, children have a chance of solving them, using syntactic and semantic cues as well as the cues provided by letter-sound relationships and letter clusters. (It is harder to judge difficulty rates at the Red Level, as so much depends on the skills children have before they start using the series. Many children will know 20–25 basic words before they begin. These words are used many times in *PM Starters One* and *Two*).
- *many opportunities for learning about directionality and punctuation, and about letter-sound relationships*: initial consonants (*h*edgehog, *h*ungry, *h*ere, *h*e), consonant blends (*br*ave, *br*own, *br*ead, *br*oken), digraphs (*th*e, *th*at, *th*is, *th*em), common suffixes (go*ing*, com*ing*, play*ing*, eat*ing*), compound words (*sunhat*, *downstairs*, *uphill*, *everyone*), regular spelling patterns (d*ay*, pl*ay*, w*ay*, m*ay*), short vowels (g*e*t, m*e*t, w*e*t, p*e*t, l*e*t, s*e*t), long vowels (s*ee*, tr*ee*, sh*ee*p, b*ee*, thr*ee*, m*ee*t), (t*ea*, s*ea*, b*ea*ch, t*ea*ch, *ea*t, r*ea*d, s*ea*l), diphthongs (c*ow*, br*ow*n, n*ow*, d*ow*n), letter clusters (l*igh*t, n*igh*t, r*igh*t). By helping children to notice letter-sound relationships teachers allow them to become code-breakers.

All this care helps teachers solve the problem of finding books that are not only *worth* reading, but also *easy* enough to read. The *New PM Story Books* are designed for children with reading abilities from five to seven years — the crucial years of reading.

Using this Teachers' Guide

Before beginning the *New PM Story Books* at Red Level children need many opportunities in the company of an adult to increase their spoken vocabulary and book experiences. At this emergent reading level the child will also practise reading using alphabet books (PM Alphabet Starters), very simple picture-caption books (PM Starters One), and simple structured pre-reading books (PM Starters Two). These books will help the child establish the right ideas about directionality and one-to-one matching of spoken and written words. Many of the high frequency basic words that the children will use in their own writing occur in these books and similar ones. When a child is sure of 20-25 basic words (I, am, is, to, the, a, etc.) then he will be ready to enjoy the *New PM Story Books*.

The teachers' guides have been designed to assist busy teachers plan and develop challenging language opportunities in their classrooms. The *New PM Story Books* are not intended to be a reading programme on their own. A wide variety of other books and materials should always be used to ensure that children succeed at each level before they proceed to the next. The ideas described in each Teachers' Guide can be adapted for other books.

There is one Teachers' Guide for each colour level:

Red   (Daisy clock levels 1, 2, 3)

Yellow   (Daisy clock levels 4, 5, 6)

Dark blue   (Daisy clock levels 7, 8, 9)

Green   (Daisy clock levels 10, 11, 12)

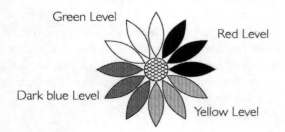

Each Teachers' Guide has suggestions and ideas for guidance in the use of the *New PM Story Books* at that level. Emphasis has been placed upon the 'Whole Language Approach' to develop the language skills of speaking, listening, reading, writing, viewing and presenting. These skills are common to all curriculum areas. Reading is not treated as a subject that stands alone.

Teacher information

This section contains notes about story content; shows the recommended reading level for each story; gives the number of running words used; comments on the types of sentence constructions that appear; and sometimes includes background information to support the teacher.

1 Creating the atmosphere

This is the 'tuning in' stage. It is the time when the teacher focuses the children's thinking on the content or concepts of the story. At this stage, related language or exciting new vocabulary can be discussed, written on the white board or sometimes acted out. In this way new ideas become familiar and the children's language is enriched.

2 Focusing on the story

This stage may take place straight after the 'tuning in' stage or may be delayed until later in the same day or even the next day. The sensitive teacher will know when the children have the right concepts and sufficient oral vocabulary. Book study is an in-depth study of the story. It is a time to follow the plot — to become emotionally involved in the tension, the climax and above all to enjoy — perhaps predict the satisfying ending.

It should be such an enjoyable experience that the children will want to read the book right through to the end all by themselves. Because new high frequency words have been introduced slowly and carefully in the books children can achieve this success.

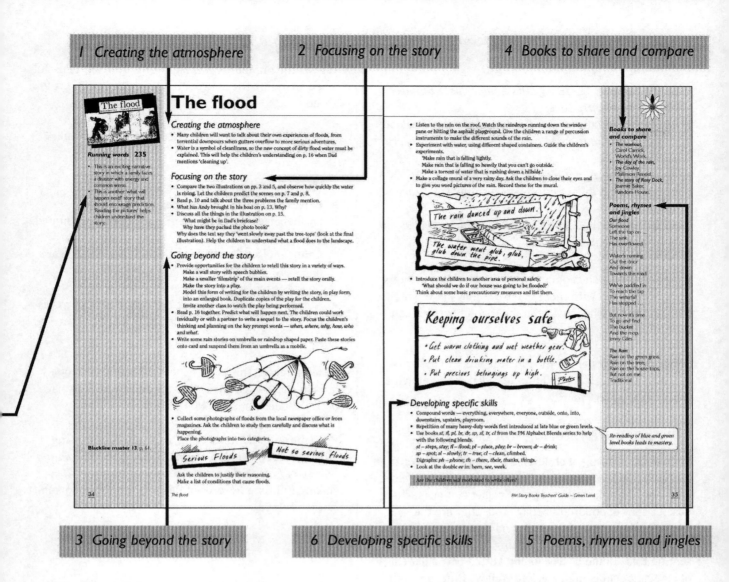

1 Creating the atmosphere   2 Focusing on the story   4 Books to share and compare

3 Going beyond the story   6 Developing specific skills   5 Poems, rhymes and jingles

3 Going beyond the story

Teachers may select from or adapt these language enrichment activities to suit the needs of their own classes. Some activities are suitable for groups of 5 – 6 children to work at together, others are for individuals. Some may even be taken with a whole class. All have been designed to develop purposeful stimulating language. They give children ample opportunity to interact verbally not only with teachers but also with one another. Some activities in science and mathematics have been included to extend children's thinking and experiences beyond the story content. The art and creative play activities will allow children opportunities to express themselves and help them to make sense of their reading.

4 Books to share and compare

These are suggested titles of books by other authors and from other publishers. Children need to have many stories read to them, often. They soon know that reading is enjoyable and will want to return to favourite books to read themselves. Occasional questions about the stories will sharpen the focus, prompt interest and talk, and ensure that children listen with understanding.

5 Poems, rhymes and jingles

Most children enjoy saying the rhythmical patterns of poems, rhymes and jingles, and singing songs. These have all been included as additional ideas to enrich each book. If they are copied onto cards or charts by the teacher, the children will have further opportunities to practise reading in a meaningful way.

6 Developing specific skills

It is important that these skills should be taught, but within the meaningful context of the child's current reading. They are not intended for teaching in isolation.

Blackline masters

Blackline masters designed to challenge children's thinking are included with the Teachers' Guides at Red, Yellow, Blue and Green Levels. Each activity is for the individual child and can be completed independently and with a sense of success.

From the very early stages the children are encouraged to use their *PM Story Books*:

- as reference material, e.g. *Mrs Spider's beautiful web, The cross-country race;*
- to follow procedures, e.g. *The island picnic, The flood;*
- to make decisions based on their own experiences, e.g. *Ben's tooth;*
- to make choices, e.g. *The clever penguins;*
- to learn about different forms of writing, e.g. *Brave Triceratops;*
- to understand how words work, e.g. *The waving sheep, The fox who foxed.*

Before the children begin work on the blackline masters discuss the sheet with them to ensure they know what they are doing, why they are doing it and how they can do it.

The blackline masters in the PM Teachers' Guides have real purpose, engaging children in independent activities that have language merit.

Language monitoring checks

Regular monitoring of children's progress is an essential part of sound teaching practice. Monitoring checks have been placed at the bottom of each page to guide teachers' observations of children's behaviours. They are the language skills, understandings and behaviours of speaking, listening, reading, writing, viewing and pre-senting that should be developing at that particular stage of language acquisition, e.g. Red, Yellow, Blue or Green Levels. They are not specific to a particular book. Some-times language monitoring checks can be used more for-mally as a checklist. (See page 42.)

The *New PM Story Books* with their rich language structures and strong storylines, provide excellent material for monitoring children's control over meaning, language structures and visual cues.

Running words

Having the number of running words available is useful when analysing the information from the reading record sheets.

Running words for these revised reading books follow these rules:

- The cover title and title page are not counted.
- Compound words are counted as one word.
- Hyphenated words, e.g. merry-go-round are counted as one word.
- Animal noises that include a vowel, e.g. Baa-baa are one word.
- Sounds such as 'sh-sh-sh' are not words.
- Numbers in numeral form, e.g. 1, 2, 3 are not words but when they are spelled out, e.g. one, two, three they are counted as a word.

Reading record sheets of the text of three books, one at each stage — Green 1, Green 2 and Green 3 — have been included on pages 44–6.

Procedures for administering and analysing running records can be found in Marie M. Clay's *An Observation Survey of Early Literacy Achievement* (Chapter 4, 'Taking Running Records of Reading text', Heinemann, Auckand, 1993).

The books at Green Level

Running words 162

- The personification of boats is traditional. This tale depends on the contrasting characters of the *Naughty Ann* and the *Jolly Jean*, described on pp. 2–3.
- Frequent repetition of familiar, heavy-duty words makes this story one that can be read with confidence.

The verse is designed for shared oral reading.

Mayday comes from the French m'aidez, meaning 'help me'.

Blackline master 1, p. 49.

The Naughty Ann

Creating the atmosphere

- Encourage the children to share their experiences of boats, e.g. fishing from rowing boats, travelling on a ferry, watching yachts on the lake or at a marina. Some children may have television or book experiences to share.
- Widen the children's vocabulary by talking about the sea, big waves, danger, Mayday calls, the smell of the sea and fish, rope, and the names of boats.

Focusing on the story

- Study the cover, the title and pp. 2–3.
  Give the children time to contrast the smart pleasure yacht with the hard-working fishing boat. Pattern the rhythm of the verse for the children, then read it together.
- Talk about the rudeness of the *Naughty Ann* on pp. 4–6. The children may want to make moral judgements about it.
- 'Read' the illustrations on pp. 7, 8 and 9 and predict the coming rough weather. Notice that the *Jolly Jean's* catch has been unloaded on the wharf (p. 8).
- On p. 11, there is a crisis. Let the children predict what will happen next.
- Enjoy the upside-down arrangement of the words on p. 12 with the children.
- Make sure the children understand how serious the danger is on pp. 14–15 and why Mayday calls are made.
- On p. 16, emphasise the main point of the story — the *Naughty Ann's* gratitude to the boat she had scorned.

Going beyond the story

- Copy the poem *Boats* by Rowena Bastin Bennett, into an enlarged book. Share the verses together and paint pictures to illustrate the book.
- Have a class yacht race. This type of activity will generate a range of language activities — discussion, decision-making, and following oral and written instructions.

- Write the yacht race rules with the children. Each boat should be given a name. Show the children how to design and make certificates for the placegetters. The race results can be written as a story in an enlarged book.
- Discuss storms at sea and on land. Extend the children's vocabulary by writing descriptive statements as you talk.
    Flashing lightning.
    Crashing thunder.
    Swirling waves.
    The thunder rumbled up and down the sky.
  The children could choose one of these statements to copy, add to it if they wish, and then illustrate it.

The Naughty Ann

- Study the illustration of the fishing boat on p. 3 and talk about the fishing gear. Ask the children to suggest what else might be taken on a boat. Some examples are a radar, ship to shore radios, wet weather clothing, emergency beacons and life jackets.

Ideas for science

- Talk about different kinds of boats and the way they move. Find photographs from magazines. Make a chart.

Muscle power	Wind power	Engine power
canoes rowing boats	sailing boats wind surfers yachts	jet boats launches ferries cargo vessels

- Make jigsaws and use them as either individual or small group reading activities.

Yacht

A yacht has sails. The wind blows into the sails.

Boat jigsaws

Match the two pieces of the jigsaw.

- Experiment with a range of materials to discover floating and sinking properties. Let the children predict the results.

Name _____

I think these things will float :
cotton reel
leaf

I think these things will sink :
bottle top
stone

The children can mark their work with a ☑ or ☒ as they do the experiment. Draw conclusions with the children about their experiments.

Developing specific skills

- Compound words — Mayday, upside.
- Endings: *ing* — fish*ing*, stay*ing*, com*ing*, go*ing*; *y* — Naught*y*, joll*y*.
- Rhymes and letter clusters — stay, away, Mayday; no, go, so; Jean, clean.

> Do the children speak clearly and confidently on selected topics, maintaining the interest of the audience?

Books to share and compare

- *Stina*,
  Lena Anderson,
  Greenwillow Books.
- *Boat book*,
  Gail Gibbons,
  A Holiday House Book.
- *Boats*,
  Anne Rockwell,
  E. P. Dutton Inc.

Poems, rhymes and jingles

Boats
The steamboat is a slow poke,
You simply cannot rush him.
The sailboat will not move at all
Without a wind to push him.

But the speedboat, with his
   sharp red nose,
Is quite a different kind
He tosses high the spray and
   leaves
The other boats behind.
Rowena Bastin Bennett

My sailing boat
Here is my little boat
Ready to put to sea.
But I must wait for the wind
   to blow
To fill the sails for me.

My sailing boat is far away
Skimming across the sea.
And I must wait for the wind
   to change,
To blow her back to me.

Running words 178

- The narrative text of this book builds on children's delight in and considerable knowledge about dinosaurs.
- The text is formally balanced on some pages to give young readers confidence (pp. 4, 8, 9, 14). Some sentences are three lines long (p. 12).

Use the pronunciation guide inside the front cover.

If each class member helps to make decisions then he or she will have a sense of ownership.

Blackline master 2, p. 50.

Brave Triceratops

Creating the atmosphere

- Ask the children to bring toy dinosaurs to school, and encourage them to share their knowledge in small groups. Display the dinosaurs, and write short descriptive statements about them.

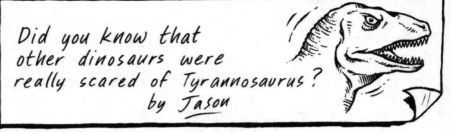

Did you know that other dinosaurs were really scared of Tyrannosaurus?
by Jason

Focusing on the story

- Look at the book's illustrations and write Tyrannosaurus Rex and Triceratops on the board. Practise saying them aloud. Notice the difference between the spelling of the written words.
- Discuss the height of Tyrannosaurus Rex — as tall as a two-storeyed house. Notice the three horns on Triceratops. These could inflict serious damage on Tyrannosaurus Rex. The point of the story will be lost if this is not understood.
- Some children may want to know the names of the dinosaurs on p. 5. Refer to the pronunciation guide on the inside cover.
- On p. 6, why doesn't Triceratops (a plant eater) run away? Let the children predict the next few pages.
- The children will enjoy chanting the last two lines of p. 16 together.

Going beyond the story

- Make masks and act out the story. Any number of children can join the fun.
- Make shadow puppets and role play the story. Use the overhead projector first to check that the outlines of the dinosaur puppets are clearly different.
- Make a pet dinosaur for the classroom. Use rolled newspaper and masking tape for the shape and papier-mâché for the outer covering.
  Decisions that must be made:
     Shall we make a dinosaur that looks like Triceratops or Tyrannosaurus Rex?
     Shall we create a new type of dinosaur? Will it have a long tail like Tyrannosaurus Rex? Will it have horns like Triceratops? How big will it be?
     Where shall we put it?
  When the dinosaur is finished, give it a name so that it can become the class mascot. Use the dinosaur as a notice board to trigger writing and speaking opportunities. Write messages to the class and hang them around the dinosaur's neck.

James is sick. He will be away from school for one week.
Who will write a letter to him?
His address is 21 Ball St.

The cloak room is messy. Please remember to keep it tidy.
Thank you,
Miss Jones.

Brave Triceratops

- Make an enlarged book. Write a description of five different dinosaurs, one description per page. Illustrate the dinosaurs using coloured paper or collage material.
- These descriptions could be written onto individual cards for the children to choose, read and illustrate.

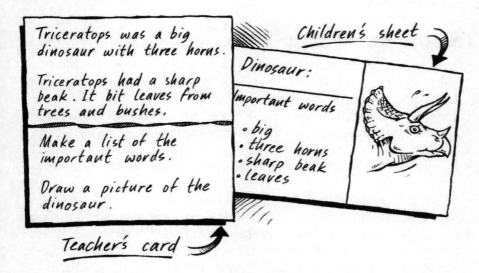

Triceratops was a big dinosaur with three horns.

Triceratops had a sharp beak. It bit leaves from trees and bushes.

Make a list of the important words.

Draw a picture of the dinosaur.

Teacher's card

Children's sheet

Dinosaur:

Important words
- big
- three horns
- sharp beak
- leaves

Show the children how to search for key information to list on their sheets.
- Cut out shapes of dinosaur body parts (such as ears, horns, tails, feet and legs) from brightly coloured felt. The children could create their own dinosaurs from these shapes which could be glued onto another piece of felt or hessian. Alternatively, cardboard shapes could be used and made into dinosaur mobiles.
- Make lists of words using the letters in — Triceratops.

Ideas for maths

- Prepare some sheets with outlines of different types of dinosaurs. Refer to *Tyrannosaurus and Triceratops* by Rupert Matthews (Picture Puffins) or *Dinosaurs A–Z guide* by Michael Rosen (Kingfisher). The children could colour these outlines, cut them out and then order them according to similar attributes, e.g. dinosaurs with strong hind legs.
  Suggest other categories for sorting the shapes:
    Order from the biggest to the smallest.
    Dinosaurs that would be bigger than an elephant.
    Dinosaurs that would be smaller than an elephant.
- Use a mathematical 'metric wheel' to measure and mark out the size of a Tyrannosaurus on the school football field. Outline the shape using brightly coloured plastic cones.
- Compare the length and height of Tyrannosaurus and Triceratops with the size of buildings, vehicles and people.

Developing specific skills

- Find the: *x* in Re*x*, si*x*, e*x*it;
          tr in *Tr*iceratops, *tr*ees;
          th in *th*e, *th*ree, *th*ump.
- Compare: Tyran*nosaur*us, di*nosaur*; th*ump*, j*ump*.

Can the children clarify or elaborate on ideas in response to questions?

Books to share and compare
- *A dinosaur named after me*, Bernard Most, Harcourt Brace Jovanovich.
- *Dinosaurs*, Michael Collins, Bookshelf Publishing Australia.
- *Patrick's dinosaurs*, Carol Carrick, Clarion Books.
- *Dinosaur bones*, Aliki, A. & C. Black Ltd.
- *Long neck and thunder foot*, Helen Piers, Penguin.

Poems, rhymes and jingles

One big dinosaur
One big dinosaur
    paddling in the sea,
Two big dinosaurs
    browsing from a tree,
Three big dinosaurs
    sharpening their claws,
Four big dinosaurs
    opening their jaws,
Five big dinosaurs
    swimming in a flood,
Six big dinosaurs
    making tracks in mud,
Seven big dinosaurs
    hiding eggs in sand,
Eight big dinosaurs
    coming in to land,
Nine big dinosaurs
    running fast for fun,
Ten big dinosaurs
    basking in the sun.

Dinosaurs are all extinct,
(They died out long ago),
But scientists have found
    their bones
And put them out on show.
Beverley Randell

Running words 175

- This is a factual book about the amazing life of the Adelie penguins in harsh and beautiful Antarctica. While it is written in narrative form, the only fictional element is the dialogue.
- Some new words are well supported by a context that is rich in familiar, heavy-duty words.

Language now flows in longer sentences. 'She stayed out at sea for days, eating and eating and getting fat.'

Through active participation in team/group situations, children learn to think critically, listen and respond to others.

Blackline master 3, p. 51.

The clever penguins

Creating the atmosphere

- Watch a short excerpt (five minutes) from a video about Adelie penguins. A good example is the documentary *Icebird* from the Wild Antarctic Collection, TVNZ. It provides a good introduction and would help the children to form concepts about Antarctica.

Focusing on the story

- Note: In Antarctica, parent penguins have to take long turns at incubation. Vulnerable eggs are never left unattended and chicks cannot survive if one parent dies at sea.
- Look at the cover, title and pp. 2 and 4. Discuss the cold pebbles that are used for nest building and the way the Adelie penguins use their whole bodies to warm the eggs.
- Discuss the little shrimp-like animals (krill) on p. 9. They are the penguins' basic food.
- Help the children read the italic type on p. 11 in a 'narrators voice', full of urgency. Teachers should pattern this to heighten the menace and the meaning.
- On pp. 14–15, observe the predatory skua gull as Mother Penguin asks "Where are my eggs?" Heightened tension here means the happy ending can be enjoyed.
- Talk about the work of both dedicated parents who have to survive in harsh Antarctica as well as care for their young chicks. Make sure the children are aware of the penguins' cleverness.

Going beyond the story

- Develop a corner of the classroom to resemble a penguin rookery. Use boxes and small tables covered with white material. Make papier-maché rocks and stones. Paint murals of scenes similar to those on pp. 6, 7 and 10. Suspend a skua gull over the landscape.
- Present the children with the following problem to solve.
  'Look at the mother and father penguins on pp. 2 and 4 of your book. Work together and make some penguins from this cardboard for our rookery.'

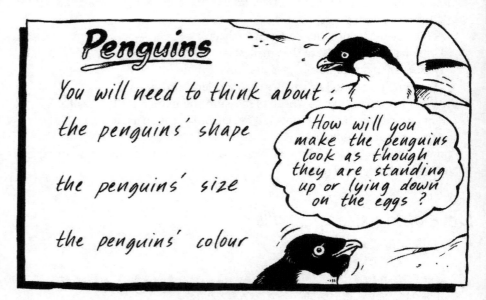

- Discover facts about penguins from the story and record them in various ways.
  a) The children could write the facts on cards to display by the classroom rookery.

The clever penguins

b) Make a large chart with the facts recorded on a computer.

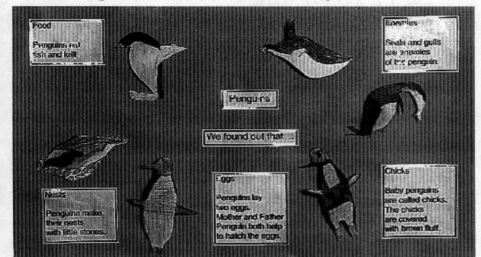

c) Many children enjoy the challenge of completing their own project booklet. These booklets could have three or four pages with topic headings on each page, e.g. Penguins' food, Baby penguins – or – leading statements, e.g. Penguins make their nests …

- Make a topic picture-dictionary of words related to facts about penguins.
- Discover different ways that birds move on land. Use a range of sources, e.g. the children's knowledge, books, photographs and videos. Build up lists of verbs.

- Read pp. 3 and 5 of the story. Talk about the importance of taking turns in social situations. Make up a class rules chart with two or three key points to reinforce this social skill. Provide simple games and activities where children take turns.

Developing specific skills

- Endings: *ed* — stay*ed*, jump*ed*, walk*ed*;
  ing — fish*ing*, eat*ing*, gett*ing*;
  er — Moth*er*, Fath*er*, clev*er*.
- Notice *ch* at the beginning of *ch*icks.
  List other known words — *ch*ildren, *ch*erries.
- Rhyming words — fat, sat. Find words in the text to rhyme with:
  may ____, hill ____, brown ____, best ____.

Are the children using appropriate reading strategies more frequently?

Books to share and compare

- *Little penguin,*
  Patrick Benson,
  Walker Books.
- *Antarctica,*
  Helen Cowcher,
  André Deutsch.
- *Penguins in the wild,*
  Cliff Moon,
  Wayland Publishers Ltd.
- *Solo, the little penguin,*
  Paul Geraghty,
  Hutchinson Children's Books.

Poems, rhymes and jingles

In icy Antarctica
In icy Antarctica
Where the snow is white
And the sea is blue
A penguin chick
Is nearly through!
The parent birds
Have warmed it well
And the chick is coming
Through its shell.
Beverley Randell

Running words 243

- This story is based on a true incident. It also explains how budgies are taught to 'talk' by patient hours of work.
- The story contains examples of 'speech' within 'speech'. Punctuation and typography help children identify these 'speech' variations. The typography suggests a different 'voice' for the budgie.

Pete Little

Creating the atmosphere

- Bring a live budgie into the classroom. Discuss how some birds can be taught to parrot words. This is not real conversation.
- Role play with the teacher being the budgie and the children asking her questions and getting a repeated response (usually inappropriate). Reverse the roles.

Focusing on the story

- Talk about pets' names, e.g. Nicola Moore's cat is called Snowy Moore. Then introduce the book. Jonathan Little's budgie is called Pete Little.
- Look at pp. 3–4. Notice Jonathan with his budgie in the conservatory and discuss his address (10 Hill Road) before reading the text.
- Read pp. 6–7. Discuss why it would be useful for a budgie to know its name and address.
- Read p. 12 and ask 'What is Mrs Grey going to do?'
  Role play the conversation between Mrs Grey and Mrs Little on p. 15. Use toy telephones and read the speech bubbles in the right order.
- Check that all the children know their names and addresses.

Going beyond the story

- Write the names of the children and their pets on a chart. Write sentences with the names, using the apostrophe correctly. Draw a picture of the pet and its owner.

The children may like to illustrate their work with photographs.

- Read some 'Lost and found' animal advertisements from the newspaper to the class. Cut them out and enlarge them for the children to read themselves. Show them how to create their own advertisements (about any lost object) to record on cassette tape or to put in the class newspaper.

Lost	Lost	Found
Lost, one blue budgie. His name is Pete. He says "Pretty Pete."	Lost, one bl___ budgie. His name is Pete. He says "Pretty P___."	Found, one red sweatshirt. It was on the swing. Come and see. Jenna.

- Give the children a strip of paper folded into three parts. Ask them to draw their own house in the middle section and to write their address below it. In the sections on either side, they can draw their next-door neighbours' homes and write their addresses. Encourage the children to think about similarities and differences in the three addresses and to talk about the sequencing of numbers in pairs. Do their streets have odd sides and even sides?

Blackline master 4, p. 52.

Pete Little

- Make a class address and telephone book. Refer to the *New PM Story Books Teachers' Guide – Blue Level*, p. 23.
- Using a disconnected telephone, demonstrate the correct skills for using a telephone. Emphasise the importance of careful dialling, careful listening and clear speaking. Let the children practise.
- Can any high achieving children find their own names and numbers in a real telephone directory and copy all the digits correctly? (Directory activities are a good way of extending the skills of bright children).
- Discuss the content of telephone conversations the children may have with family members. Role play these situations, then record the content in speech bubbles on a cyclostyled sheet.

- Re-read the New PM Story Book *Fire! Fire!* Notice the cell-phone used by Mr Brown and the pilot. Discuss the conversations in the speech bubbles. Make 'cell-phones' at the woodwork bench or in the art and craft corner.
- Make a bird in a cage. Using light card, cut an outline of a bird. Using firm paper, draw and cut the shape of the cage. Fold it and cut to make the rungs of the cage. Open it out and slot the bird in position.

- The more advanced learners could work in pairs to find information about: birds that are kept in cages; or birds' beaks, and the food they eat.

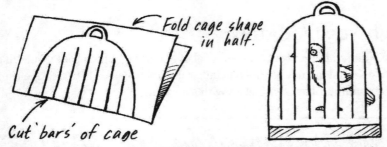

Developing specific skills

- Children should now be using their knowledge of known words to master unknown words: blew, — flew; look — book; some, one — someone; Mr — Mrs; Ann — Anna; cake, make — take.
- Use books *cl, fl, tr, gr, ph, sm* from the PM Alphabet Blends series to help with these words.
  cl – *cl*ever; *fl* – *fl*ew; *tr* – *tr*ee; *Gr* – *Gr*ey; *ph* – *ph*one; *sm* – *sm*iled.

Do the children read for meaning and understanding?

Poems, rhymes and jingles

Pussycat
Pussycat, pussycat,
   where have you been,
Licking your lips
   with your whiskers so clean?
Pussycat, pussycat,
   purring and pudgy,
Pussycat, pussycat,
   WHERE IS OUR BUDGIE?
Max Fatchen

Running words 223

- There is a strong logical flow to this story. The cramped interior on p. 2 and the colder weather (shown by autumn leaves and warm scarves) are two reasons for house-hunting. The three bears hunt for a home to match their needs.
- Longer sentences can now be mastered, e.g. 'In the morning, Father Bear and Mother Bear and Baby Bear went into the forest to look for a new home'.

> *Children clarify their thinking when they are directed to focus on specific points.*

> *This type of activity helps children draw on their personal background, knowledge and experience.*

Blackline master 5, p. 53.

House-hunting

Creating the atmosphere

- Read the poem *A new friend* by Majorie Allen Anderson. Talk about moving house — packing up furniture and other belongings, and the excitement and apprehension involved.

Focusing on the story

- The cover should give the children clues about the story. Discuss the 'For Sale/Sold' notice and the laden car. Produce the six earlier Bear books and recall Baby Bear's fondness for honey, Father Bear's delight in fishing, and Mother Bear's scarves.

   'Have they packed their frying pan?'
   'Where have we seen those baskets before?'

> *Reading is about being interested. Encourage such delights and do not rush this process.*

- Read pp. 3 and 5 and let the children discuss the Bears' problem of having to move from their home in a tree trunk to a warmer cave now that winter is approaching. Talk about the cramped room shown on p. 2.
- Pages 7–9 appeal to children's logic.
- The children will enjoy the illustration and text on pp. 10–11 when they see the beehive and spot the 'For Sale' notice in the background. They will also enjoy having their predictions confirmed, overleaf.
- After reading pp. 13 and 15, ask the children why the new home is more suitable than the Bears' old home. List all the points.

   Mother Bear liked … Father Bear liked … Baby Bear liked …

Going beyond the story

- Ask the children to draw or make a model of a house in which they would like to live. They should include as much detail as possible. Make a list of all the things they like about it. Share these ideas with a partner.

- Read the poem *A new friend* again. Ask the children how the little boy peering through the fence would be feeling. List his emotions. They could illustrate their individual copies of the poem and then write two or three ways to make a new neighbour feel welcome.
- Carefully select some 'House for Sale' advertisements from the newspaper to read to the children.
   Discuss the important elements that should be included. The children could work in pairs to write a 'For Sale' advertisement for the Bears' new home. Read pp. 11–15 to find the important information.
- Discussions about the seven Bear family books could lead to the following activities.

a) Each child chooses their three favourite Bear books and makes a booklet about them. Show the children how to set out the contents page.

They could write the main ideas of each book selected and draw a picture of the best part. Justification for their selection of text could be either verbal or written 'I liked the book *Blackberries* because …'

b) Develop simple character studies with the children. Read the books together to find the information about Baby Bear.

The children could then work in pairs or small groups to find things to record in a similar way about Father Bear and Mother Bear.

Ideas for science

- Read p. 5 again. Relate the meaning of the text to the illustration. Note the colour of the leaves on the trees. Talk about seasonal changes.
  Draw pictures of the four seasons on a long strip of paper that has been folded into four parts. Finally join the strip to make a circle to show the on-going cycle.

Developing specific skills

- Analyse *moose*. 'Why isn't it *mouse*?'
  Look at the double *oo* in m**oo**, t**oo**, z**oo**, t**oo**th, m**oo**se.
- Compound words — beehive, hillside, nowhere, downstairs, inside.
- Contractions — let's, that's, it's, here's.

Do the children display confidence in taking risks and making approximations in reading and writing?

Books to share and compare

- *Moving,*
  Michael Rosen,
  Penguin.
- *New big house,*
  Debi Gliori,
  Walker Books.
- *Moving Molly,*
  Shirley Hughes,
  The Bodley Head.
- *A house for Lily Mouse,*
  Michelle Cartlidge,
  Methuen.
- *Moving house,*
  Barbara Taylor Cork,
  Conran Octopus Ltd.

Poems, rhymes and jingles

A new friend
They've taken in the furniture;
I watched them carefully.
I wondered, 'Will there be a child
Just right to play with me?'

So I peeked through
The garden fence
(I couldn't wait to see).
I found the little boy next door
Was peeking back at me.
Majorie Allen Anderson

Whirling leaves
Like a leaf or feather
In the windy, windy weather
We whirl around,
And twirl around
And all fall down together.

Candle-light

Story by Beverley Randell Illustrated by Genevieve Rees

Running words 229

- The links with other stories about Ben are strong — *Ben's Teddy Bear, Ben's treasure hunt, Ben's dad, The best cake*. Discussing these links is an enjoyable literary experience.
- In this book there are many phrases that indicate the passing of time, for example, 'At bedtime ..., But before he got into bed ..., And then ..., ... after the story ...' These phrases, which many children will be starting to use in their own writing, lead to the construction of longer sentences with the rhythms of literary English.

Take these opportunities to enliven guided reading and make it a literary experience.

Blackline master 6, p. 54.

Candle-light

Creating the atmosphere

- Bring to class a variety of candles and/or illustrations including candles. Discuss their uses — for decoration, celebration and light. Let the children talk about their own experiences of birthday cakes, family dinners etc.
- Light a candle and talk about the flickering flame, the wick and the wax. Observe the melting wax.

Reinforce safety rules.

Focusing on the story

- Look at the cover illustration and talk about why Mum is reading Ben's bedtime story by candle-light. List these ideas. Observant children may notice that Mum is reading *Dogger* by Shirley Hughes (The Bodley Head) and might remember that Mum bought it at the fair in *The best cake*. Promise to read this book to the children later.
- Pages 5, 7, 9 show a logical development. Notice that throughout this book safety with matches and candles is carefully emphasised — Mum supervises on every page.
- The tune for the verse on p. 11 is *Here we go round the mulberry bush*.
- The tune for the verse on p. 15 is *Oranges and lemons*. Draw the children's attention to the words 'sang a song'. Sing the verse together.
- Make sure the children know why Ben was disappointed on p. 13 and why Mum kindly put out the light on p. 15, to let him continue enjoying the candle-light.

Going beyond the story

- Write a simple book review retelling the main events of the story. Include an additional section where the child gives his/her opinion about the story.

- Read reassuring stories about night-time to the children.
  Write stories about the night, the darkness, the moon, the stars, the shadows and the uncertainty associated with them.
- Make shadow puppets of characters from a favourite story. Practise retelling the story first by using an overhead projector. Then perform the play behind an illuminated screen, using a powerful light.
- Read the poem *My shadow* by Robert Louis Stevenson. Demonstrate to the children that shadows move and change, by exploring the following activities.
  On a sunny day, trace a friend's shadow using chalk.
  Try this again at a different time of day.
  Move hands to make animal shapes, using the overhead projector.
  Move to music as a happy shadow, a tired shadow, or a dancing shadow.
  Mime shadows — follow a partner's movement and copy it.
- Provide the opportunity for high achieving children to learn the oral skills of persuasion and argument. Teach them how to present a very simple debate to the class. Use the topic 'Torches and candles make the best lighting for our homes'.

- Write poems about candles. Help children extend their vocabulary as they watch a candle burn.

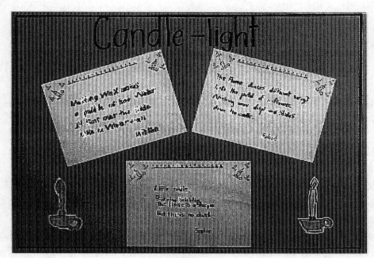

- Draw and colour birthday cakes decorated with candles. Cut out these pictures and arrange them on a wall frieze to show the children's birthdays.
- Make candles similar to those in *The Christmas tree* (New PM Story Books – Blue Level). Use art and craft materials to make the holders for the candles.

clay pots   tin foil plate   egg cartons

Ideas for science

- Discuss power failure.
  'What could have caused it?
  How should we be prepared for it?'
  Discuss safety rules for using electricity and candles. List them on a chart.
  Record these ideas in a class book *Keeping ourselves safe*.
- Select from, and develop, these related science activities:
  Stars and the moon
  Light
  Torches

Developing specific skills

- Compound words — tea-time, bedtime, bedroom, bathroom, candle-light.
- 'She sang a song.'
- Blow it out — blew it out.

Do the children display more skill in reasoning and predicting?

Books to share and compare

- *Can't you sleep, little bear?*, Martin Waddell and Barbara Firth, Walker Books.
- *Tucking Mummy in*, Morag Loh, Ashton Scholastic.

Poems, rhymes and jingles

Candlelight
Flickering candle
in the darkness
Glistening,
glowing flame,
Silently whispering
brightly burning
dancing in the night
Magic shadows
from the candlelight.
A.C. Lundon

My candles (finger play)
Look! My hand is my candlestick
And my fingers are candles bright.
Five fat candles
With flickering flames
Shining and dancing, a lovely sight.
Now watch and I will blow
Out each shining flame will go.

My shadow
I have a little shadow
    that goes in and out with me
And what can be the use of him
    is more than I can see
He is very, very like me
    from the heels up to the head;
And I see him jump before me,
    when I jump into my bed.
Robert Louis Stevenson

Running words 197

- This is the sixth book about Ben. It is a straight forward story, understood and enjoyed by six and seven year olds because they know exactly what Ben is going through — his experience is their experience.
- This familiar situation is told in narrative form. Reading is not always about finding out, it is often about discovering one's own experiences in print.

Ben's tooth

Creating the atmosphere

- Read together the story *Tooth fairy magic* by Joanne Barkan (Scholastic Inc).

Focusing on the story

- Study the cover illustration and the title. Observant children will notice the tooth in Ben's apple and the gap in his teeth.
- Read p. 3. Let the children discuss their feelings and they will relate to Ben's excitement.
- Study the illustration and text on pp. 4–5, and recall Mrs Green the teacher from an earlier story *Ben's dad*. When the children look at the little box in the teacher's drawer many will spot the favourite story *Mog the forgetful cat* on her desk (read this to the children later).
- On pp. 7–11, Mum shares Ben's obvious delight and plays along with the tooth fairy idea, in spite of Ben's doubts.
- Read pp. 9–16. The story is carefully open-ended allowing for the two possible interpretations. Those children 'in the know' should be encouraged not to shatter their peers' ideas:
  Note on p. 9 'The tooth fairy *may* come …' and on p. 13 'Will she? Or won't she?'

Going beyond the story

- Ask the children to pretend to be Ben and write a letter to his father (who is away at sea) telling him about the exciting events of the past day — losing his first tooth.
- Invite a dental therapist to visit the classroom and speak to the children about why first teeth come out. Before the dental therapist visits prepare a list of questions the children would like answered. Write these questions on separate cards so that the children can practise speaking clearly.
- Some children may like to keep a tooth diary to record the important events as they occur.

- Make a time-line of events that happened in Ben's day.

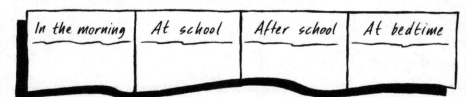

- Study the six 'Ben' stories. Pose questions to the children to direct their reading.
  'What do you notice about the covers on all the 'Ben' books?
  Who is Ben's teacher? Which stories do we see her in?
  Find the names of all the books Ben and his Mum like to read.'

Blackline master 7, p. 55.

Ben's tooth

Ask six children to separately write a brief summary of a different 'Ben' story and illustrate it. Paste each page to the sides of a brightly painted box to create a six-sided 'Ben' story box.

- Read a fairy story to the children in which a fairy brings a gift, e.g. *Cinderella*, *The three wishes*.

Ideas for science

- Find pictures of animals' teeth. Make lists of these animals with photographs or illustrations of the different kinds of teeth.
  'A rabbit has very big, sharp teeth in the front for cutting grass.
  A shark has huge numbers of razor sharp teeth for grabbing fish.'

Ideas for maths

- Make a pictorial graph about missing first teeth.
  Collect the data from a group of children.

Analyse the information with the children, e.g. 'On 12 July, Tom had lost 5 teeth. He had lost the most teeth. Nick hadn't lost any teeth.'
- Keep a picture record of missing first teeth.

Developing specific skills

- Observe things about the *internal* parts of words — *or, morning, story, stories; too, tooth; sleep, Green, see.*

Do the children display an increasing independence in reading a variety of books?

PM Story Books Teachers' Guide – Green Level

Books to share and compare

- *My teeth,*
  Ron Thomas and
  Jan Stutchbury,
  The Macmillan Company.
- *What do the fairies do with all those teeth?*
  Michel Luppens,
  Scholastic Canada Ltd.
- *The crocodile's toothbrush,*
  Boris Zakhoder,
  Marguerite Rudolph and
  Wallace Tripp,
  Kingswood Surrey.
- *Tooth fairy magic,*
  Joanne Barkan,
  Scholastic Inc.

Poems, rhymes and jingles

But then
A tooth fell out
and left a space
so big my tongue
can touch my face.

And every time
I smile, I show
a space where something
used to grow.

I miss my tooth
as you can guess …
but then
I have to brush
ONE LESS.

Tim's loose tooth
Tim had twenty teeth on
  Tuesday …
Ate a toffee, got a fright!
Tim had twenty teeth on
  Tuesday …
Tim had nineteen,
  Tuesday night.
Beverley Randell

At this level the more that children can develop insights into code-breaking, the better.

Running words 212

- This book is about the life of the garden orb-web spider. Mrs Spider's voiced thoughts are fictional, but apart from this the story is strictly scientific — fact, not fiction.
- The events of this story are set out in clear time sequence. This structure allows for a great deal of prediction.

> *Pleasure increases exposure to print and this increases learning.*

> *More opportunities for the children to observe spiders' webs will help them to develop the scientific skills of comparing, contrasting and predicting.*

Blackline master 8, p. 56.

Mrs Spider's beautiful web

Creating the atmosphere

- Take the children out into the school environment to find an orb-web spider's web. Talk about the size, shape, pattern and delicate construction. Make this visit early in the morning when webs are freshly made and drenched with morning dew.

Focusing on the story

- Study the cover illustration and the title. Compare the size of the web with the size of the spider.
  Read p. 2 and make sure the children understand why Mrs Spider made her beautiful web.
  Note the correct sequence of web making on pp. 2–10.
  The first line of the web is carried by the wind. Strong construction lines are anchored to the bushes. The central coil is made and finally the outer coil is added, and made sticky.
  Notice how hard Mrs Spider worked, not giving up until the task was finished.
- Note that 95 per cent of the words in this book first appeared in earlier stories. Reading mastery comes from re-reading stories independently for pleasure. It is through re-reading a favourite story again and again that consolidaton of skills takes place.

Going beyond the story

- Extend and enrich the children's listening and speaking vocabulary by recording their observations of spiders' webs on a chart. Select a word or phrase to highlight.

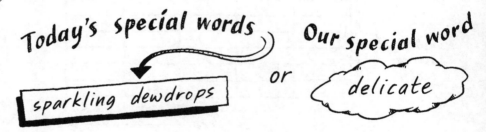

- Make a 'facts' book or chart from the information in the story book. Direct the children to search for and list information from key questions.
  'How long did Mrs Spider take to make her web?
  What did Mrs Spider have for dinner?'
- Show the children how to make up their own 'spider' questions. Record these questions and answers on separate cards for the children to use as an additional reading activity (finding the matching pairs). Put a matching picture as a clue on each pair of cards.

- Talk about how Mrs Spider had to be very patient as she waited for the fly.
  Make a list of the many times we have to wait patiently in everyday life.
  'Sometimes we have to wait for a long time at the supermarket checkout, at the doctor's, or for a bus.'

- Use a greasy crayon to draw the web of an orb-web spider on light card or hessian, (copy it from pp. 4–9 of the story). With a large darning needle and wool, sew over the web shape using running stitches.
- Make a large wall display similar to the cover design. Make a web from string and hang it from the bushes. Make a spider from black paper. Attach explanatory sentences from the many observations that have been made.
- Weaving activities.
  a) Fold in half a piece of paper (300 mm x 200 mm). Cut strips in wavy lines to within 30 mm of the top. Open the paper and weave strips of coloured paper or light card in 'basket weave' style.

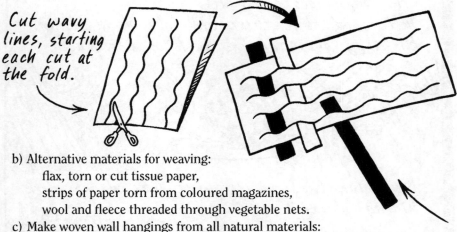

Cut wavy lines, starting each cut at the fold.

  b) Alternative materials for weaving:
     flax, torn or cut tissue paper,
     strips of paper torn from coloured magazines,
     wool and fleece threaded through vegetable nets.
  c) Make woven wall hangings from all natural materials:
     raw wool, flax, dried seaweed, lichens, coloured autumn leaves.

Ideas for maths

- Symmetrical patterns.
  Study the shape of the web and the shape of the spider. Fold in half a piece of paper. Use a greasy crayon and draw half of the web or spider, beginning at the centre as shown.

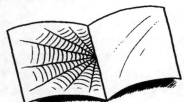 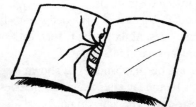

Fold the paper in half again and press hard. Open it to reveal a symmetrical web or spider.

Discover other examples of symmetry in the classroom or school environment.

Developing specific skills

- Children should have a growing sight vocabulary of heavy-duty words:
  again, want, very, round, worked, there, something, now, more;
  and less heavy-duty words: broken, dinner, hid, beautiful, wind, blew.
- Punctuation — stressed words in bold print
  — inverted commas show direct speech
  — three dots to link ideas.
- Rhyming words — my, by, fly; at, sat; where, there; blew, flew.

Can the children read silently for a purpose?

Books to share and compare

- *The Kuia and the spider,*
  Patricia Grace,
  Longman Paul.
- *Zoe's webs,*
  Thomas West,
  Ashton Scholastic.
- *The very busy spider,*
  Eric Carle,
  Philomel Books.
- *Spider's web,*
  Christine Back and
  Barrie Watts,
  A. & C. Black Ltd.
- *Spiders,*
  Gail Gibbons,
  A Holiday House Book.

Poems, rhymes and jingles

Lady Spider
Please take care my lady spider
To weave your web
A little tighter
Spider babes are very small
And look like nothing else at all
So tiny they could slip and fall
Through webs on ceilings,
Floor and wall
Please take care my lady spider
To weave your web
A little tighter.
Lillian M. Fisher

Fairy Cobweb
I saw a fairy's cobweb
Hanging in a tree
A cobweb full of diamonds
As glittering as could be
I saw it in the morning
But later in the day
The fairy took her diamonds
And now the cobweb's grey.

Ten little garden snails

Running words 101
(Read twice) 202

- The life cycle of the snail is emphasised by the structure of this cyclic book which never truly ends (like the garden snail).
  The book is scientifically accurate as well as being fun.
- Prediction is helped in this story by three things: scientific accuracy; rhymes triggering the correct numerals; and illustrations which indicate where the snails will go or what will attack them.

> *Motivate children to show curiosity in the natural environment.*

> *Talk about the word 'thrush' (called a spotted bird in the story).*

Blackline master 9, p. 57.

> *Shared observations will deepen the children's understanding and increase their curiosity.*

Creating the atmosphere

- Ask the children to bring some garden snails to school. Make a list of the places where the snails were found. Make conclusions from this list.

Hannah found three snails in the flax bush.
Robert looked under a sack by the wheelbarrow.
He found lots of snails.
Julie said that there are lots of snails in the long grass at the back of her place.

We think that snails must like damp, dark hiding places.

Focusing on the story

- Read the title together and count the snails on the cover.
- 'The old grey gate' on p. 2 is a poetic way of stressing that snails like damp shady neglected corners. Children need to understand that snails have to remain moist. They will sometimes dehydrate and die in the sun even when they are locked away inside their shells.
- Read pp. 6–10. At night the hedgehogs hunt for snails as they both leave their hiding places. At dawn the thrush eats snails, cracking their shells open on a stone. Hens eat snails too.
- Snails are hermaphrodites as shown on pp. 12–16 and lay eggs a few centimetres underground. The eggs on pp. 1 and 16 are the same size as real snail eggs.

> *The triumphant ending to this story appears only when the title page is studied and the book is re-read.*

- The title page has been numbered to allow children to 'go back to page 1'.
  The story should be read at least twice at the first sitting, following the instructions on p. 16. In spite of all their enemies, snails never disappear!

Going beyond the story

- Increase the children's knowledge of snails. Listen to snails eating cabbage. Observe the movement of snails. Place a snail on a glass plate and view it moving from above and below the plate.
  Encourage the children to ask questions. Record these questions for discussion with the class or a group, as well as giving instant responses to individuals.
- From the story, list some of the snail's enemies.
  'What other enemies might the snail have?
  How does the snail protect itself from enemies?'

Ten little garden snails

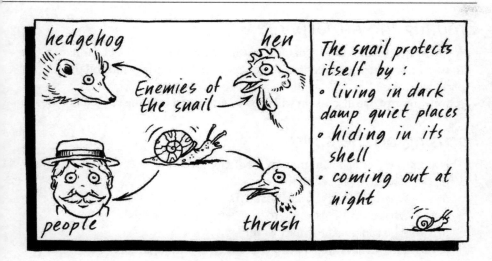

- Use magnifying glasses to study the colour and markings on the snail shell and body. Discuss camouflage.
  Copy these markings onto a prepared outline shape of a snail.
- Lend the children an inexpensive camera to photograph snails.
  Make decisions together about what to photograph, e.g. a snail eating lettuce or a snail curling into its shell.
  Enlarge the photographs and mount them attractively. They can be used for a variety of purposes — group discussion, one-to-one assessment with the teacher, displayed in an enlarged book or on a facts board.
- Prepare individual project booklets for the children to complete in a few days. Number the pages and include a contents page. Children could finish incomplete sentences. 'Snails live … Snails eat …
  Snails are eaten by…'
- Find out about other animals which have a protective shell or a protective covering. This can be an individual research project for advanced children. Reinforce the importance of gathering information from a range of sources.
- Use a large glass or plastic container to create a natural environment for a snail. Keep snails for a few days and observe them closely. Write stories or poems on snail-shaped paper.

Ideas for maths

- Make an enlarged book of the story with a double page spread for each verse. Discuss the way the numbers reduce by two and highlight them. The children could draw, cut and paste the snails onto the brightly painted background.
- Sing the verses of *Ten little garden snails* to the tune of the nursery rhyme *Baa baa black sheep*.
- Set up a snail trail with a real snail. Find out how long it takes a snail to move a distance of 10 centimetres.

Developing specific skills

- Focus on these rhyming words and listen to their impact: gate/eight; sticks/six; more/four; dew/two; sun/one.
- Punctuation — three dots … means there is more to come.

Are the children developing expressive oral reading using punctuation?

Books to share and compare

- *The snail's spell*, Joanne Ryder, Frederick Warne & Co.
- *Snails: Life cycle books*, Althea, Longman.
- *Snails*, Jennifer Coldrey, Picture Puffins.

Poems, rhymes and jingles

The snail
All across the garden wall
Silvery and bright
There's a line where a snail
Took a walk last night.
He came from the rockery
For something to eat.
And that would be
His foot-marks
If a snail had feet.

Have you ever seen a snail
Going off for walks,
With his house on his back,
And his eyes on stalks?
Well, when he has finished
He rolls them in his head
And goes inside his tiny house
And tucks himself in bed.
Rodney Bennett

The snail house
It hasn't any windows,
It hasn't any door,
Although it has a ceiling,
It hasn't any floor.
'Twas built without a builder,
A hammer, brick or nail,
Because you see,
This little house,
Belongs to Mr Snail.

Running words 222

- This narrative story unfolds logically. The school bus broke down, it was towed away, it was offered for sale, which gave Mr Biggs an idea … and onto the satisfying ending.
- Such logical development lies at the heart of thought, language and reading. Children are encouraged to think by being allowed to think.

> *Children should learn how to respond to text, to think critically and to process information.*

The little red bus

Creating the atmosphere

- Invite someone who has mechanical or carpentry skills into the classroom to talk to the children about his/her tools, e.g. spanners for shifting nuts, oil to make parts move freely.
  A lively informative discussion will provide an insight into the story that follows.

Focusing on the story

- This story is full of opportunities for prediction:
    p. 2 — What will happen to the bus?
    p. 4 — Where is the tow truck taking it?
    p. 6 — What is Mr Biggs going to do when he buys the bus?
    p. 8 — Who can guess the next word?
    pp. 10, 12 — What will happen when the tyres and engine are fixed, the beds are built, the sink put in and the caravan is painted?
    pp. 14, 16 — Where do you think the family will go for their holiday?

Going beyond the story

- Follow up the ideas presented in *Creating the atmosphere*.
  Develop the concept of word relationships:
    A saw is for sawing wood.
    A hammer is for hitting nails.
    Screws and nails join wood together.
    A rule is for measuring.
    A spanner is for turning nuts and bolts, etc.
  Let the children handle these tools and write a sentence about two or three of them. Illustrate the sentences to make a chart, concertina book or an enlarged book.

- Read to the class *The way I go to school* (PM Starters One, Nelson Price Milburn). Discuss the reasons why children have different modes of transport to school. Ask each child to write and draw about the way they travel to school, and make a wall display.
- Make contact with schools in other areas, e.g. an urban school could contact a rural school. Regular letter writing to a pen-pal could provide many new exciting learning opportunities. Contact with other schools via e-mail and telephone audio conference technology would provide even more opportunities for personal involvement.

> *Reinforce social courtesies.*

- Invite the owner of a caravan to bring the vehicle to school. The children could work in pairs to prepare questions to ask the owner.
  Collate these questions and let the children practise saying them before the visit to increase their confidence.

Blackline master 10, p. 58.

- Make a list, with the children, of all the essential items a caravan should contain. The children could work in pairs and draw or paint pictures of the caravan. Each pair could discuss the list of essential items and between them choose the five most important ones.

The little red bus

To complete the activity each pair could share their picture with the rest of the class, justifying their choice of the five essential items.

- Organise the children into small groups of three or four.
  Ask them to talk about their different holiday experiences. Help the speakers to shape their ideas by asking *where, who, why, when, what* and *how*.
  Encourage the listeners to focus on the key question words.
- Show the children postcards received from someone who has been on holiday. Write a postcard to a friend. Send a message, write the address, design a stamp on one side and illustrate the reverse side.
- Talk about the Biggs family working together. Encourage the children to discuss work they like to do with their family. Follow up this discussion with writing and drawing.
- Suggest this debate topic for high achieving children, 'Caravans are best for holidays'. Encourage the audience to listen carefully to the reasons presented by the speaker. They may like to give their own opinions later.
  The speakers' ideas could be recorded on a large chart.

- Make a list of related words: caravan, campervan, camper, mobile home, trailer home. Extend this activity with high achieving children. Help them use dictionaries to find the meanings. Compare and discuss the dictionary meanings.

Developing specific skills

- Find – *ay* in d*ay*, holid*ay*, aw*ay*.
- Use the blends *br–, tr– dr–, sl–* to decode *br*oke, *br*akes, *tr*uck, *dr*iving, *sl*owly.
  Read the books *br, tr, dr, sl* from the PM Alphabet Blends series to improve skills.
- Study these and other two-syllable words in the story: going, little, children, engine.

Can the children discuss book characters, scenes and episodes with understanding?

> *Encourage children to listen and to interact appropriately in group situations.*

> *This is an oral exercise (clap the syllables).*

Books to share and compare

- We're off:
  Verses on the move,
  Compiled by Brian Thompson,
  Puffin.
- *Postman Pat wins a prize*,
  John Cunliffe,
  André Deutsch.

Poems, rhymes and jingles

Caravan
When I've saved up
(I know I can)
I'm going to buy
A caravan.
I'll have my stove
And bed with me
When I go camping
By the sea.
Beverley Randell

Running words   208

- This story is a dramatic narrative, very closely based on a true incident. It is important for children to realise that a real fox will play dead in exactly this way. Foxes behave in intelligent ways to avoid capture, and this behaviour has entered many folk stories.
- Predictability and logic are an essential part of this story — every page has clues that lead to the events on the next page.

Talk about the importance of detail in illustrations.

Blackline master 11, p. 59.

The fox who foxed

Creating the atmosphere

- Develop the theme of the story — foxes, their habits and intelligence — by playing part of the video *The urban fox*, or by reading and discussing the story *Proud Rooster and the Fox* by Colin Threadgall, (Julia MacRae Books).

Focusing on the story

- Discuss the title first. 'What does it mean?' Some children may be more familiar with the American term 'played possum' which means the same thing. The title, *The fox who foxed*, links with 'He was foxing!' (p. 11) and the final line of the book '… but I foxed him.' This preliminary understanding is important and will lead to more insight when the story is read.
- Read pp. 2–15. As the children finish reading each page ask them: 'What do you think will happen now?' There is a good chance of a correct prediction each time.
- Read p. 7 aloud. The children should say the sound, not the name of the letter 'k', and thus imitate the noise made by the distressed hens.
- Make sure the children stress the word **foxed** as shown on p. 16 to bring out the meaning. This last line should sound triumphant, and must be read with full understanding.

Going beyond the story

- Read the well-known story *The gingerbread man* to the children. Compare the cunningness of that fox with the one in the story book. Summarise the key points with reasoning and justification.

> **The gingerbread man**
>
> The fox pretended to be friends with the gingerbread man. He gave him a ride across the river on his back. The gingerbread man was feeling pleased with himself. But the sly fox ..
>
> **The fox who foxed**
>
> The fox pretended to be dead when the farmer hit him.
>
> The former was feeling pleased with himself. But the sly fox - - - - -

- Make a list of animals and their homes.
    'A dog lives in a kennel.
    A guinea pig lives in a hutch.'
Extend this list to other domesticated animals.
    'A budgie lives in a cage.
    A horse lives in a stable.
    A pig lives in a sty.'
Animals that live in the wild.
    'A fox lives in a den.
    A bear lives in a cave.
    A beaver lives in a lodge.
    A penguin lives in a rookery.'

Charts

or wall stories

or concertina charts

The fox who foxed

- Use the ideas from p. 30 in a variety of reading and matching activities.

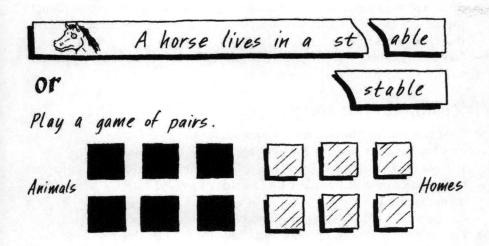

or

Play a game of pairs.

Animals   Homes

- Extend the children's research skills by asking them to compare the similarities and differences between the fox and the dog. Begin by recording the children's present knowledge and listing their questions.

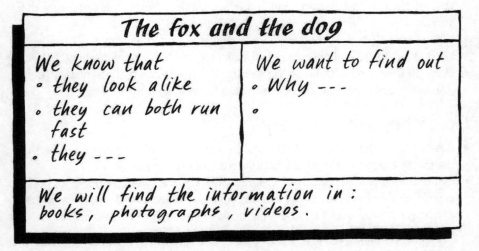

Present the information on a chart, in a book or as a model.
- Ask the children to illustrate four important parts of the story in sequence. Find appropriate sentences in the story book to copy beneath each picture.
- Make a diorama of the scene that shows the farmer, fox and hens.
  Write a brief explanation of the scene on a computer, giving reasons for the characters' actions.

> *Give children the opportunity to choose their own methods of publishing and presenting information.*

Developing specific skills

- Look at 'x' as in fox, box, six, fix, next, Rex.
- Common endings: farm, farmer; jump, jumped; fox, foxed, foxing; open, opened.
- Notice the sounds of these short vowels.

    a — ran, man; fat, cat.
    e — Ben, hen; get, let.
    i — big, pig; hid, did.
    o — fox, box; stop, top.
    u — sun, fun; but, shut.

Can the children spell many words correctly?

Books to share and compare

- *The farmyard cat in trouble,* Christine Anello, Ashton Scholastic,
- *Harquin, the fox who went down to the valley,* John Burningham, Cape.
- *Fox's dream,* Tejima, Philomel Books.
- *The fox went out on a chilly night,* Peter Spier, Dell.

Poems, rhymes and jingles

Foxy
Foxy's creeping round the farm
Trying to get the chickens.
Up pops Farmer Jones with his gun.
Bang! bang! Look at Foxy run!
He runs away and hides —
And home goes Farmer Jones
Then old Foxy he creeps back
To get those chicken bones.

Running words 235

The island picnic

Creating the atmosphere

- Study a photograph or large illustration of a person rowing a small boat (facing the stern). Observe the actions of the rower. Notice how rowing makes the boat move backwards.
- Talk about the uses of such a small craft, e.g. transport to and from larger boats and the shore, fishing in calm waters.

Focusing on the story

- The cover and the title page give clues about the story.
  'What has gone wrong on the title page? How do the children know?'
  If they have spotted this, they will notice the trailing rope on p. 6 and anticipate the events on pp. 8–9. Introduce the idea that rivers have currents (which flow down the river to the sea).
- The separation of Sally's parents is evident in the first sentence on p. 3.
- Look at pp. 4–5. Discuss the word 'island' and the fact that they rowed up river against the flow of the current.
  'Dad is tying a knot, but …'
- On pp. 6–7, why don't Dad and Sally notice the disaster until it's too late? Make sure the children 'read' the illustration before the crisis overleaf.
  Discuss the fact that Dad and Sally remembered their life jackets but forgot their sunhats.
- When reading pp. 8–9, encourage 'crisis voices' — avoid flat tones.
- Look at pp. 14–15 and observe how the picture and text work together.
- On p. 16 the moral of the story is important – anyone can make a mistake, even a grown-up. Sally and Dad are now planning to avoid another mistake.

Going beyond the story

- Read a picnic story or poem to the children. Ask them why we have picnics. Use the theme *enjoyment* to illustrate different types of picnics.
- Plan a class picnic in the school grounds or nearby park. Ask grandparents or elderly neighbours to attend by sending them an invitation. The picnic may have a theme, e.g. 'The mad sunhatters picnic day'. The design and wording of the invitation should reflect the theme.

Blackline master 12, p. 60.

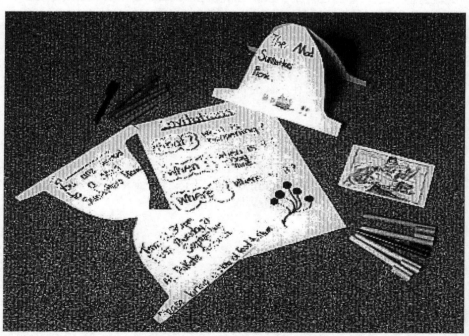

The island picnic

- Talk about making mistakes and learning from them. Model some examples for the children to discuss.

Problem	Solution
Dad tied the boat up but it wasn't a good knot.	Dad has learnt how to tie a very good knot.

Problem	Solution
Mrs Bryant's car stopped on the way to school.	Mrs Bryant checks the petrol every day now.

Ask the children to write about their own mistakes and the solution to the problem. Share these ideas in a positive manner with the whole class.
- Talk about rivers and streams and the obvious dangers they present. Children need to be aware of swift flowing currents and the hidden dangers on the riverbed.

Make a large mural for the children to colour and paste on 'dangerous items.'

Fast current in the middle — snags and logs — River bed — hidden boulders — rusty cans and broken glass

- Practise tying knots. Invite a Sea Scout or Guide leader to demonstrate two or three simple, basic knots.
- Learn to tie shoe laces.
- Decorate boxes and tie coloured string or wool around them with knots and bows.
- Copy the verses of the well-known song *The teddy bears picnic* onto a wall chart. The children could use paint for the background and collage material for the teddy bears. Sing the song often, using the wall chart to learn the words by heart.
- Develop an understanding of water safety and boat safety to include in the class book, *Keeping ourselves safe*.

Rules :
- Always wear a life jacket.
- Sit in a small boat.
- Don't jump up and down.
- Learn to swim.... etc.

Developing specific skills
- Compound words — something, runaway, tea-towel, today.
- Long words that can be guessed from context plus knowledge of the first syllable: *sat* — *Sat*urday, *sand* — *sand*wich, *run* — *run*away.
- New awareness of syllables.
  Clap the three syllables in run–a–way, sand–wich–es, Sat–ur–day.
- Revision of endings — *ed*: ti*ed*, open*ed*, shout*ed*, wav*ed*, bark*ed*.

Do the children make logical attempts at spelling unknown words?

Books to share and compare
- *Lily's picnic,*
  Paul Rogers,
  The Bodley Head.
- *This is the bear and the picnic lunch,*
  Sarah Hayes and
  Helen Craig,
  Walker Books.
- *The teddy bears' picnic,*
  Jimmy Kennedy,
  Green Tiger Press.

Poems, rhymes and jingles
A picnic
We had a picnic
  by the lake
We ate
  some sandwiches
  and cake.
We munched
  and crunched
  till we were through.
We liked the taste
The ants did, too.
Sandra Liatsos

Where go the boats?
Dark brown is the river,
Golden is the sand,
It flows along for ever,
With trees on either hand.

Green leaves a-floating,
Castles of the foam.
Boats of mine a-boating –
Where will all come home?

On goes the river,
And out past the mill,
Away down the valley,
Away down the hill.

Away down the river,
A hundred miles or more,
Other little children
Shall bring my boats ashore.
Robert Louis Stevenson

Running words 235

- This is an exciting narrative story in which a family faces a disaster with energy and common sense.
- This is another 'what will happen next?' story that should encourage prediction. 'Reading the pictures' helps children understand the story.

The flood

Creating the atmosphere

- Many children will want to talk about their own experiences of floods, from torrential downpours when gutters overflow to more serious adventures.
- Water is a symbol of cleanliness, so the new concept of dirty flood water must be explained. This will help the children's understanding on p. 16 when Dad mentions 'cleaning up'.

Focusing on the story

- Compare the two illustrations on pp. 3 and 5, and observe how quickly the water is rising. Let the children predict the scenes on p. 7 and p. 8.
- Read p. 10 and talk about the three problems the family mention.
- What has Andy brought in his boat on p. 13. Why?
- Discuss all the things in the illustration on p. 15.
    'What might be in Dad's briefcase?
    Why have they packed the photo book?'
Why does the text say they 'went slowly away past the tree-tops' (look at the final illustration). Help the children to understand what a flood does to the landscape.

Going beyond the story

- Provide opportunities for the children to retell this story in a variety of ways.
    Make a wall story with speech bubbles.
    Make a smaller 'filmstrip' of the main events — retell the story orally.
    Make the story into a play.
    Model this form of writing for the children by writing the story, in play form, into an enlarged book. Duplicate copies of the play for the children.
    Invite another class to watch the play being performed.
- Read p. 16 together. Predict what will happen next. The children could work invidually or with a partner to write a sequel to the story. Focus the children's thinking and planning on the key prompt words — *when, where, why, how, who* and *what*.
- Write some rain stories on umbrella or raindrop shaped paper. Paste these stories onto card and suspend them from an umbrella as a mobile.

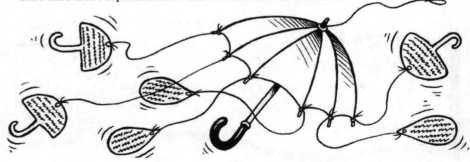

- Collect some photographs of floods from the local newspaper office or from magazines. Ask the children to study them carefully and discuss what is happening.
Place the photographs into two categories.

Serious Floods   Not so serious floods

Ask the children to justify their reasoning.
Make a list of conditions that cause floods.

Blackline master 13, p. 61.

The flood

- Listen to the rain on the roof. Watch the raindrops running down the window pane or hitting the asphalt playground. Give the children a range of percussion instruments to make the different sounds of the rain.
- Experiment with water, using different shaped containers. Guide the children's experiments.
    'Make rain that is falling lightly.
    Make rain that is falling so heavily that you can't go outside.
    Make a torrent of water that is rushing down a hillside.'
- Make a collage mural of a very rainy day. Ask the children to close their eyes and to give you word pictures of the rain. Record these for the mural.

The rain danced up and down.

The water went glub, glub, glub down the pipe.

- Introduce the children to another area of personal safety.
    'What should we do if our house was going to be flooded?'
    Think about some basic precautionary measures and list them.

Keeping ourselves safe

∘ Get warm clothing and wet weather gear.
∘ Put clean drinking water in a bottle.
∘ Put precious belongings up high.

Photos

Developing specific skills

- Compound words — everything, everywhere, everyone, outside, onto, into, downstairs, upstairs, playroom.
- Repetition of many heavy-duty words first introduced at late blue or green levels.
- Use books *st, fl, pl, br, dr, sp, sl, tr, cl* from the PM Alphabet Blends series to help with the following blends.
    st – *st*eps, *st*ay; *fl* – *fl*ood; *pl* – *pl*ace, *pl*ay; *br* – *br*own; *dr* – *dr*ink;
    sp – *sp*ot; *sl* – *sl*owly; *tr* – *tr*ee; *cl* – *cl*ean, *cl*imbed.
    Digraphs: *ph* – *ph*one; *th* – *th*ere, *th*eir, *th*anks, *th*ings.
- Look at the double *ee* in: b*ee*n, s*ee*, w*ee*k.

Are the children self motivated to write often?

Re-reading of blue and green level books leads to mastery.

Books to share and compare

- *The washout,* Carol Carrick, World's Work.
- *The day of the rain,* Joy Cowley, Mallinson Rendel.
- *The story of Rosy Dock,* Jeannie Baker, Random House.

Poems, rhymes and jingles

Our flood
Someone
Left the tap on …
The sink
Has overflowed.

Water's running
Out the door
And down
Towards the road.

We've paddled in
To reach the tap
The waterfall
Has stopped …

But now it's time
To go and find
The bucket
And the mop.
Jenny Giles

The Rain
Rain on the green grass,
Rain on the tree;
Rain on the house-tops,
But not on me.
Traditional

Running words 265

- This story is based on a real incident. It is a long story but the children will want to go on reading to the end because of the tension.
- Enjoyment and satisfaction will be increased when the flowing rhythmic language in this book is read aloud.

Blackline master 14, p. 62.

Pepper's adventure

Creating the atmosphere

- Keep a pet mouse in a cage in the classroom (even for a short time).
  Talk about pet care — food, water, exercise. Children should learn that mice are gregarious and use the sense of *smell* as well as *hearing* and *sight*.

Focusing on the story

- Read p. 3 and talk about the two mice.
  'Why were the names Pepper and Salt chosen?'
  Discussion will help children master the names.
- On p. 5, why would the mice be happier in the bigger cage?
- Make sure the children know why Mum said "Don't take them outside".
  They will see why Nicky's behaviour on p. 7 was so foolish and be able to predict p. 9.
- Discuss the problem on p. 9, and possible ways of recapturing a lost pet mouse.
- Help the children see that Mum's and Sarah's ideas were good on p. 13. The smell of the old cage would mean security to a lost mouse.
- On p. 14, the children will enjoy spotting the tiny mouse on the right of the flower bed as it approaches the old cage. A happy ending to the story can now be anticipated.
- If necessary, pattern the last sentence of p. 16 for the children, emphasising the last word. This will make the meaning clear.

Going beyond the story

- Read several stories about mice to the children. Have these books readily available in a display area for them to read by themselves. Make a 'mouse trail' of the books that have been shared.

Frederick by Leo Lionni 11 July

John the mouse who learned to read by Beverley Randell 12 July

Some children may like to keep their own reading record. Encourage this positive reading behaviour.
- Read poems regularly to the children. Have copies available so they can select and paste their favourite ones in an illustrated booklet of mouse poems. Collage illustrations will add to the very personal nature of this anthology.
- Read a well written copy of the traditional story, *The town mouse and the country mouse* to the children. Discuss the adventure of the country mouse and compare it to Pepper's adventure.

▷ *The adventures of two mice*

The country mouse ..... Pepper

What was the country mouse afraid of?
Was Pepper afraid of anything?
How do we know that mice feel scared?

Pepper's adventure

- Design a 'Lost' advertisement for Pepper (refer to p. 16 of this guide).
- Talk to the children about the concept of time-lines. Demonstrate how they can record their own day at school on a time-line. Read the story book again. Record the important events on a chart. The children can now work individually or with a partner to make a time-line of *Pepper's adventure*.
- Ask the children to find words with opposites in this story. List them on a chart. The children could role play pairs of opposites for the rest of the group to guess. Select some examples of opposites that would be easy to illustrate. Discuss why some words would be more difficult to draw than others, e.g. bring, take.
- Read p. 5 of the story book together. Ask the children to design and make a 'pretend' cage for Pepper and Salt. Give the children criteria to follow in their planning.

A cage for the mice

- The cage must be big enough for two mice.
- The cage should have exercise equipment.
- The cage must be a safe place for the mice.

When the children present their models to the class they should be able to explain and justify the above criteria.

- Lend the children a camera to photograph the class pet mouse. Ask them to write a class book about caring for mice. The children will need to make decisions about the photographs based on their story planning words — *how*, *where*, *when*, *what* and *who*.

Use the photographs to illustrate the book.

> *Some of these blends are very rare even at this level of reading.*

Developing specific skills

- Use books *br, cr, fl, pl, fr, gr, wh, th* from the PM Alphabet Blends series to help with the following blends.
  br – brown, bring; cr – crying; fl – flower; pl – played, places, pleased; fr – from; gr – grass; wh – white, wheel; th – there, they, that.
- Opposites — pleased, sorry; inside, outside; old, new; do, don't; lost, found; here, there; open, shut; bring, take.

Are the children beginning to re-read their own writing for meaning and spelling accuracy?

Books to share and compare

- *Nicholas, where have you been?*,
  Leo Lionni,
  Alfred A. Knopf.
- *Mouse count*,
  Ellen Stoll Walsh,
  Harcourt Brace Jovanovich.
- *Five mice and the moon*,
  Joyce Dunbar,
  Orchard Books.
- *House mouse*,
  Barrie Watts,
  A&C Black.
- *Harvest mouse*,
  Jennifer Coldrey,
  André Deutsch.

Poems, rhymes and jingles

Wanted

I'm looking for a house
Said the little brown mouse,
     with
One room for breakfast,
One room for tea,
One room for supper,
And that makes three.
One room to dance in,
When I give a ball,
A kitchen and a bedroom,
Six rooms in all.
Rose Fyleman

Running words   262

- This is the third book about Jessica, Daniel, Gran and Dad, the farming family. Compare the three books and enjoy the consistent landscape.
- Reasoning is built into every page of this story which encourages children to think.

The waving sheep

Creating the atmosphere

- Study a large coloured photograph or illustration of sheep being shorn. Talk about the fact that sheep are bred for their heavy, woolly coats. Sheep sometimes get off balance and become cast on their backs. They'd die of starvation if not righted.

Focusing on the story

- On p. 2, the recent rain is significant (refer to p. 8).
- Study the landscape picture on pp. 4 and 5 and compare it with *Cows in the garden* and *The house in the tree*.
    'What is Daniel pointing at?'
  Help the children notice the two tiny waving legs by the fence.
- Read pp. 6–9. The pictures make the sheep's problem clear (it may have been struggling for some hours already and is very wet and heavy).
- Why are Gran and Daniel wearing helmets on p. 11?
- On pp. 14–15, discuss the important fact that the sheep had to be propped up for some time as it would have difficulty controlling its numb legs.
- Read p. 16. Saving the sheep was a satisfying adventure. Help the children to say Daniel's words in just the right way, stressing **saved**.

Going beyond the story

- Retell the story in three parts. Make a large wall display with three headings (see below). Decorate the illustrations with collage material. Include speech bubbles where appropriate.

> *This type of activity helps children to look more closely at the story structure — the problem, the climax, the resolution.*

The waving sheep

What was wrong?   What they did about it.   How it came right.

1
The sheep was on its back.

2
Jessica and Daniel pushed and pushed the heavy sheep.

3
Gran helped and they pushed the sheep up on its legs.

- Make a large web chart of different types of farms and different kinds of farm animals. Find newspaper, magazine or brochure photographs to provide additional opportunities for questioning, reasoning, predicting and comparing.

Blackline master 15, p. 63.

> *Show the children how to search for and extract information from a variety of sources.*

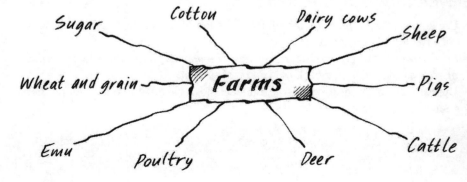

The waving sheep

- Read stories to the children about farming activities — milking, haymaking, shearing, mustering. Use photographs and documentary videos to extend understanding.
- Extend the children's learning opportunities by making contact with schools in other areas via e-mail and audio conference technology (refer to p. 28, *The little red bus*).
- Invite someone with a spinning wheel to demonstrate this skilled art to the class.
- Make wall hangings by weaving different types and thicknesses of wool.

Children should learn to think critically about language and meaning as they listen to, and view, demonstrations.

- With the help of older students or adults, teach the children how to knit a square 10 cms x 10 cms. Join these squares together to make a wall hanging or a doll's quilt.
- Make 'wool' spider webs using forked twigs and wool of different colours and textures.

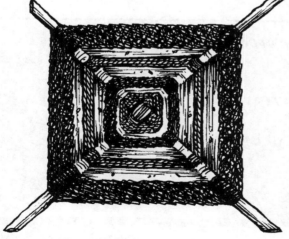

Developing specific skills

- Verbs — tense endings.
  — *ed*: wav*ed*, walk*ed*, push*ed*, help*ed*, start*ed*, sav*ed*, smil*ed*.
  — *ing*: wav*ing*, bring*ing*, milk*ing*, com*ing*, sitt*ing*.
- Rhyming words — add new words: wave, save, —; right, light, night, —; it, sit, —; now, cow, —; will, hill, —; all, ball, —; get, let, pet, —.
- Stress the words in bold print.

Can the children find and use information from a range of sources, e.g. books, pictures and videos?

Books to share and compare

- *Farm boy, city girl*, Dorothy Butler and Lyn Kriegler, Ashton Scholastic.
- *Emma's lamb*, Kim Lewis, Walker Books.
- *Animal world: Cows*, Tessa Potter and Donna Bailey, Steck-Vaughn Company.
- *Argyle*, Barbara Brooks Wallace, Abingdon Press.

Poems, rhymes and jingles

I held a lamb
One day when I went visiting,
A little lamb was there,
I picked it up and held it tight,
It didn't seem to care.
Its wool was soft and felt so
   warm —
Like sunlight on the sand,
And when I gently put it down
It licked me on the hand.
Kim Worthington

Running words 244

- This is the third book about Tim, Michael, Anna and their teacher Mrs Hill.
  The story is about running races, friendship and being in touch with one's feelings.
- This book introduces a new skill — how to interpret a *picture map*. Another new skill is reading words in capitals, e.g. START and FINISH on p. 3, GO on p. 9.

Blackline master 16, p. 64.

> *Seize every opportunity for children to explore language and to extend their vocabulary.*

The cross-country race

Creating the atmosphere

- Organise the children into teams (of mixed gender) and have some races in the school grounds. Talk about the races beforehand:
  'What will happen? Who will win?'
- Back in the classroom, write a shared story (teacher and children) about these races. In this way, the children can see that every race or sporting event follows a 'story form', the problem of who will win and its solution.

Focusing on the story

- Look at the cover title and pp. 2–3. Explain cross-country racing to the children.
- On pp. 4–5, take time to trace the route the runners will follow. Read the phrases and tie them to the illustrations. Meaning matters! Then read the text.
- Identify Tim, Michael and Anna in the illustrations on pp. 3 and 7.
- Read pp. 8–9. Make sure the children understand the phrase 'class after class'.
- 'Tim wanted to win. He **was** winning.' These sentences on p. 10 are very important. If the children understand Tim's emotions here they will understand the nature of his sacrifice on p. 12.
- Read p. 12. Interesting discussion should arise from the fact that Tim's desire to help his friend was stronger than his desire to win the race. This is a story about a value judgement.
- Help the children understand how Michael felt on p. 14 — he wanted Mr James to know about Tim's sacrifice.
- On p. 16, it is clear that Tim had lost the race but had won something else — a strong friendship. Talk about friendships that sometimes last for ever.

Going beyond the story

- Read the story again to the children from p. 10. Display the following chart.

Tim stopped to help Michael.
Tim did not win the race.

Tim was a _____ friend.

Encourage the children to suggest words that bring out the full meaning of friendship in this situation.
- High achieving children could extend this discussion further by reading, hearing or talking about acts of bravery and courage where people put others' needs before their own.
- Study the cross-country course in the story book on pp. 4–5. Discuss with the children the idea of planning their own cross-country or obstacle course.
  Ask the children for their suggestions.
    'What should we do first?
    Where will the course go?
    How can we tell if the course is too easy or too hard?'

40

- Involvement in the planning will include activities such as: floor maps, using large sheets of paper, wooden blocks and felt pens; stand-up pictures in an old tray; and wall plans.

Explore the important positional language 'over …, behind …, across …, by …, round …' and record these phrases.

- Make posters for the Principal's office, the school library or the school newsletter advertising this special occasion.
- Make the plan of the cross-country race into a maths game with dice numbered one to six, and cue cards.

- Discuss the importance of keeping fit and having a healthy body. Ask the children to plan some fitness activities for the next day. Model some ideas.

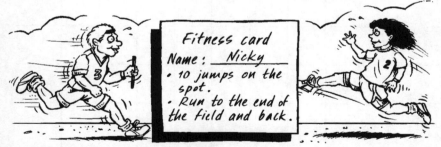

Developing specific skills

- Prepositions and their meanings — over, up, behind, by, round, past, across, back, before, on, off.
- Opposites — start, finish; fast, slow; over, under; won, lost; win, lose; get up, fall down; first, last; before, after; in, out; stop, go.
- Capital letters are often used in signs.
  Compare Start with START, Finish with FINISH, Go with GO.

Do the children express their feelings and ideas through various media, e.g. mime, movement, art, writing?

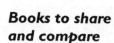

Books to share and compare

- *The big mile race*, Leonard Kessler, Greenwillow Books.

Poems, rhymes and jingles

Cross country
Cross country, cross country
Off we go!
Running round the tall trees
All in a row …

Cross country, cross country
I'm having fun.
Running here … by myself?
Where is everyone?

Cross country, cross country
I can see my friends
Running up and down the hill!
Will it never end?

Cross country, cross country
I've had enough!
Running … to … the … finish
    line
Puff!
    Puff!
        Puff!
Jenny Giles

Language monitoring checks

Green Level Skills, understandings and behaviours	Jenna	Rael	Adam	Luke				
Speaking / Listening								
• Speaks clearly and confidently on selected topics, maintaining the attention of the audience	✔	✔	✔	✔				3/11
• Clarifies or elaborates on ideas in response to questions	✔	✔	✗	✗				4/11
• Uses appropriate reading strategies more frequently								
• Reads for meaning and understanding								
• Displays confidence in taking risks and making approximations in reading and writing								
• Displays more skill in reasoning and predicting								
• Displays increasing independence in reading a variety of books								
• Can read silently for a purpose								
• Is developing expressive oral reading using punctuation								
• Can discuss book characters, scenes and episodes with understanding								
• Can spell many words correctly								
• Makes logical attempts at spelling unknown words								
• Is self-motivated to write often								
• Is beginning to re-read own writing for meaning and spelling accuracy								
• Finds and uses information from a range of sources, for example: books, pictures, videos								
• Expresses feelings and ideas through different media, for example: mime, movement, art, writing								

Column group headings: **Speaking / Listening**, **Reading / Writing**, **Viewing / Presenting**

General comments (Date all observations)

Language monitoring checks

	Speaking / Listening		Reading / Writing		Viewing / Presenting		

Green Level

Skills, understandings and behaviours

• Speaks clearly and confidently on selected topics, maintaining the attention of the audience							
• Clarifies or elaborates on ideas in response to questions							
• Uses appropriate reading strategies more frequently							
• Reads for meaning and understanding							
• Displays confidence in taking risks and making approximations in reading and writing							
• Displays more skill in reasoning and predicting							
• Displays increasing independence in reading a variety of books							
• Can read silently for a purpose							
• Is developing expressive oral reading using punctuation							
• Can discuss book characters, scenes and episodes with understanding							
• Can spell many words correctly							
• Makes logical attempts at spelling unknown words							
• Is self-motivated to write often							
• Is beginning to re-read own writing for meaning and spelling accuracy							
• Finds and uses information from a range of sources, for example: books, pictures, videos							
• Expresses feelings and ideas through different media, for example: mime, movement, art, writing							

General comments (Date all observations)

Reading record

Name: _____   Age: _____   Date: _____

Text: *The clever penguins* Green 1. R.W. 107

Summary _____

_____

_____

_____

Page		E	S.C.	Errors MSV	Self corrections MSV
3	The Penguins had a nest				
	with two big white eggs in it.				
	Mother Penguin sat on the eggs day after day.				
	Father Penguin went fishing.				
5	One day Father Penguin came back.				
	"Here I am," he said to Mother Penguin.				
	"You will be hungry. I will sit on the eggs, now.				
	Off you go."				
6	Mother Penguin went down the hill				
7	and into the sea to eat fish.				
9	Mother Penguin went out to sea.				
	She stayed out at sea for days,				
	eating and eating and getting fat.				
	Father Penguin stayed on the eggs.				
11	*Look out, Mother Penguin!*				
	Look out for the hungry seal!				
	*Seals like to eat **fat** penguins.*				

Reading record © Nelson Price Milburn. This page is copyright free.

Reading record

Name: Age: Date:

Text: *The little red bus*   Green 2.   R.W. 114

Summary

Page		E	S.C.	Errors MSV	Self corrections MSV
2	One day the little red school bus broke down on the way home. The mothers and fathers had to come in cars to get the children.				
4	The next day a truck towed the little red bus back to the garage. The children went to school in a new yellow bus.				
6	Mr Biggs went to look at the old bus. He looked inside the engine. "I can make it go again," he said. "I'm good at fixing engines. I will buy this old bus."				
8	Mr Biggs came driving slowly home in the old bus. "Look!" he said to Mrs Biggs and the two little Biggs. "This little red bus is going to be …				
10	… a **caravan!**"				

Reading record

Name: _____   Age: _____   Date: _____

Text: *Pepper's adventure*   Green 3.   R.W. 104

Summary _____

_____

_____

_____

Page		E	S.C.	Errors MSV	Self corrections MSV
3	One day Dad came home with two pet mice in a little cage. Sarah loved them. She called the brown one Pepper and the white one Salt.				
5	Dad made a big new cage for Pepper and Salt. It had a wheel and a ladder and a room upstairs. Sarah played with the mice a lot, and so did Nicky from next door. "Don't take them outside," said Mum.				
7	But one day Nicky **did** take Pepper outside. "No! Don't do that!" said Sarah. "Bring Pepper back inside!" But Nicky put Pepper down on the grass to see if he liked it, and …				
9	… Pepper ran away!				

Reading record

Name: Age: Date:

Text: Green   R.W.

Summary

Page		E	S.C.	Errors MSV	Self corrections MSV

Using the Blackline masters

Before using each Blackline master prepare the children as follows:

Blackline master 1   *The Naughty Ann*
- Read each verse with the children. Predict the missing words.
- Ask the children to use the words in boxes to complete the writing. Cut out each verse. In the correct order of the story-line, paste the verses into individual booklets. Illustrate the verses and give the booklet a new title.

Blackline master 2   *Brave Triceratops*
- Study the illustrations of Tyrannosaurus Rex and Triceratops, in the story book. Identify the characteristics of each dinosaur.
- Read the lists of 'helpful words' together.
- Ask the children to draw their pictures in the boxes before they begin writing their descriptions.

Blackline master 3   *The clever penguins*
- Read pp. 11 and 13 of the story. Discuss the fact that seals are a constant danger to penguins in the Antarctic.
- Have available several copies of other New PM Story Books that show birds and animals in similar situations, e.g. *Lizard loses his tail, Tiger, Tiger, Pussy and the birds, Hermit Crab.*
- Ask the children to choose two books to write about and illustrate.

Blackline master 4   *Pete Little*
- Discuss what might be said in the telephone conversation.
- Write two or three of these ideas on a chart.

Blackline master 5   *House-hunting*
- Revise contractions and compound words within the meaningful context of the story book.
- Discuss the layout of the Blackline master. 'Part 1 is about … Part 2 is about …'
- Direct the children to read pp. 11 and 13 of their story book to find the answers to Part 3.

Blackline master 6   *Candle-light*
- Look closely at the story book cover and the repeated illustration on p. 14. Discuss favourite stories.
- Let each child choose a book from the classroom library.
- Read through the Blackline master with the children and ensure they understand the directions.

Blackline master 7   *Ben's tooth*
- Discuss dental care and healthy eating.
- Study the two illustrations of Ben on the Blackline master and read the sentences together.
- Discuss some answers to the two questions before the children proceed independently.

Blackline master 8   *Mrs Spider's beautiful web*
- Study the illustrations closely on pp. 3 to 9.
- Ensure the children can identify the six different stages of web-making.

Blackline master 9   *Ten little garden snails*
- Read the first sentence to the children.
- Discuss some answers to the four key questions.
- Talk about how these ideas could be used in the story.

Blackline master 10   *The little red bus*
- Show the children how to search for key information in the text of the story book.
- Encourage them to draw detailed illustrations related to the instructions.

Blackline master 11   *The fox who foxed*
- Revise common letter clusters, e.g. –at, –ill. Read the first sentence with the children. Let them choose the word, from the box, that retains the sense of the text.
- Ask the children to complete each sentence.

Blackline master 12   *The island picnic*
- Study the sketches. Read the clues together, predicting the missing words.
- Ensure the children know how to complete a crossword.

Blackline master 13   *The flood*
- With the children, read the text in each of the four boxes.
- Discuss the concept of order.
- Read and interpret the instructions together.
- Give each child a strip of firm paper onto which the four boxes can be pasted, in the correct order.

Blackline master 14   *Pepper's adventure*
- Study the blends in the box. Use PM Alphabet Blends books to revise words that begin with these sounds.
- Read the text of the Blackline master with the children. Support their attempts to use the context and the blends to decode the unknown words.

Blackline master 15   *The waving sheep*
- Ask the children to read aloud the words in the box. Listen to the final sounds. Observe the common spelling of these endings.
- Read the words in number 2 aloud. Guess each new word from the illustration and sound. Discuss the initial letters.

Blackline master 16   *The cross-country race*
- Prepare the Blackline masters beforehand by pasting each one onto a firm piece of paper.
- Ask the children to read pp. 4 and 5 of their books before cutting and colouring each piece of the jigsaw puzzle.

My name is _____

Today is _____

| today | am | mast | new | clean | stay | blue | can |

The *Naughty Ann* was painted blue.

The *Naughty Ann* was clean and n _ _.

The fishing boat (the *Jolly Jean*)

was not so new and not so cl _ _ _.

"You smell of fish. I'm going away.

I do not like your smell t _ _ _ _.

I'm going!" said the *Naughty Ann*.

"I'm going out to sea, I _ _!"

A big green wave came rushing past.

It hit the yacht and broke her m _ _ _.

The *Jolly Jean* knew what to do.

She saved the yacht all painted bl _ _.

"I like the smell of fish today.

I'm sorry that I did not st _ _.

"Thank you," said the *Naughty Ann*.

Please forgive me if you c _ _."

My name is _____

Today is _____

Tyrannosaurus Rex had _____

_____

_____

_____

_____

_____

Helpful words

| teeth | sharp | fierce | eat | dinosaur |

Triceratops had _____

_____

_____

_____

_____

Helpful words

| horns | three | sharp | brave |

Brave Triceratops © Nelson Price Milburn. This page is copyright free.

My name is _____

Today is _____

Birds and animals try to keep themselves safe.

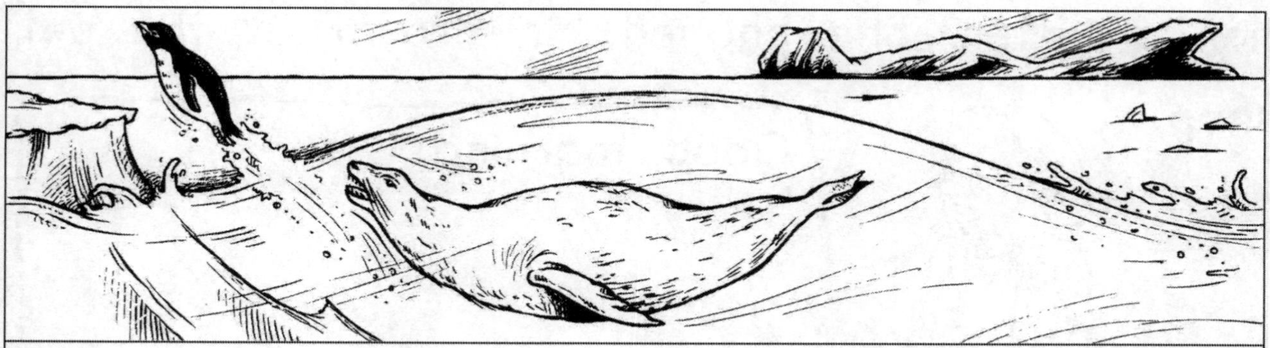

Mother Penguin jumped away from the s_ _ _.

Read, write and draw about other animals
that kept themselves safe.

Draw
Write

Draw
Write

My name is _____

Today is _____

It was Sarah's birthday. Mum wanted to buy her a kitten. She phoned Mr Brown at the pet shop.

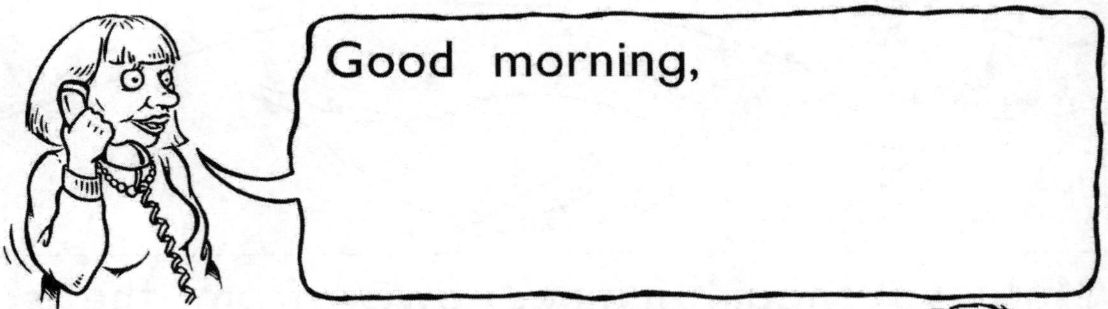

Good morning,

Mr Brown had a little grey kitten for sale.

Draw and write what might happen next.

My name is _____

Today is _____

1. Put these words in the right spaces.

| That's | Here's | Let's | It's | Let's |

"_____ go and find a new home,"

said Mother Bear.

"_____ not a home for bears,"

said Father Bear.

"_____ a home for a rabbit."

"_____ a big warm cave,"

said Mother Bear.

"_____ move in today."

2. Find the two small words in each big word.

hillside   hill _____

beehive   _____ _____

nowhere   _____ _____

downstairs   _____ _____

inside   _____ _____

3. Mother Bear liked the new big _____.

Baby Bear liked _____.

Father Bear liked _____.

My name is _____

Today is _____

Mum read Ben a favourite story
at bedtime. It was called *Dogger*.

My favourite story is . . .
"_____"

My story is about . . .

_____

_____

_____

I like this story because . . .

_____

This is a picture about the best part
of my story.

My name is _____

Today is _____

Ben looks after his teeth.

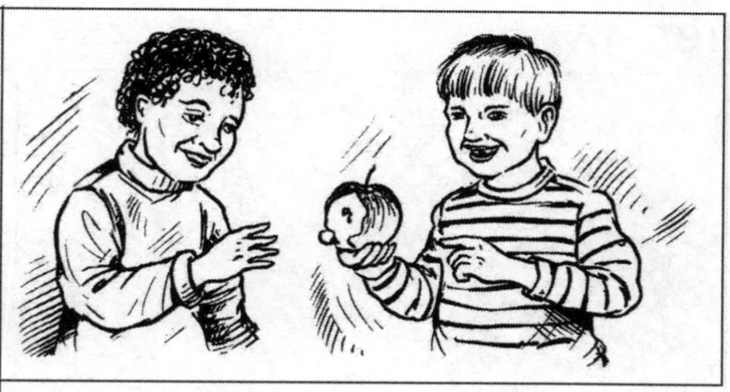

He cleans his teeth before he goes to bed.

He eats an apple with his lunch at school.

How do you look after your teeth?

_____

_____

_____

What foods do you like best?
All of them are good for your teeth.

apple

carrot

celery

coconut

milk

banana

cheese

_____

_____

_____

My name is _____

Today is _____

Draw a plan to show how Mrs Spider made
her web

1.

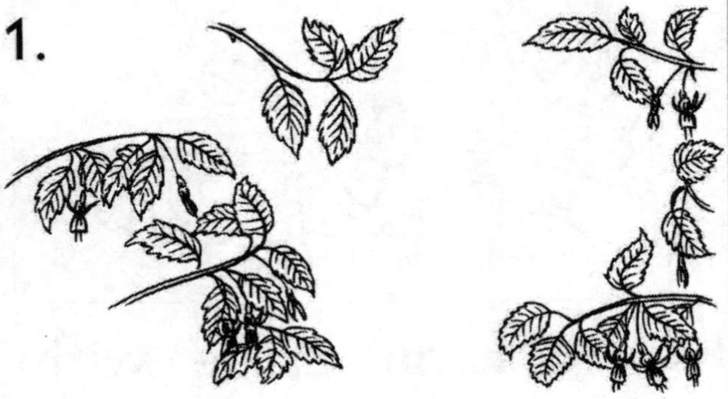

First _____

_____

2.

Next _____

_____

3.

Then _____

_____

4.

After that_____

_____

5.

When she had done
that she _____

6.

Last of all_____

_____

My name is _____

Today is _____

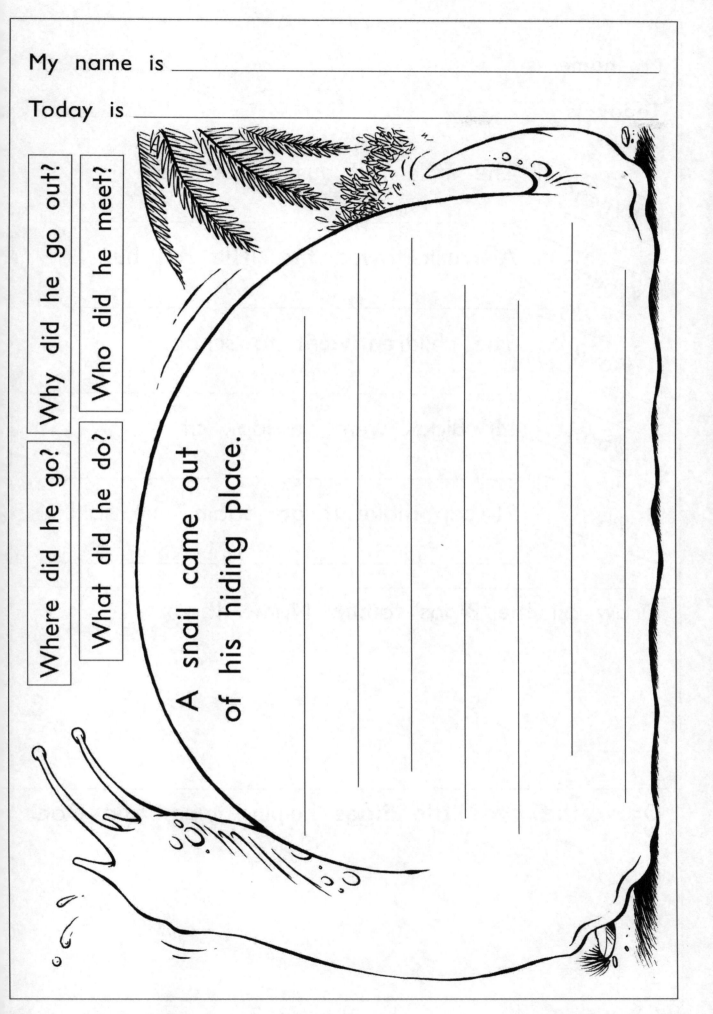

Where did he go? Why did he go out?

What did he do? Who did he meet?

A snail came out of his hiding place.

My name is _____

Today is _____

When?	The little red bus broke down _____ .
Where?	A truck towed the little red bus _____ .
How?	The children went to school _____ .
What?	Mr Biggs went to look at _____ .
Why?	"I can make it go again," he said. _____ .

Draw all the Biggs family. Name them.

Draw the two little Biggs helping Mum and Dad.

The little red bus © Nelson Price Milburn. This page is copyright free.

My name is _____

Today is _____

Put the best word in each space.

Mr Fox went to find a _____

little hen.

| cat |
| sat |
| fat |

He went down the _____

to the farm.

| will |
| fill |
| hill |

Mr Fox jumped at the door

of the hen-house and _____ in.

| ran |
| man |
| fan |

"A _____ is in my hen-house,"

shouted the farmer.

| box |
| fox |

He ran into the hen-house

with a _____.

| stick |
| kick |

He _____ the door.

| but |
| shut |

The farmer hit Mr Fox

and he fell _____.

| brown |
| down |

"Good. I _____ him. He's dead,"

said the farmer.

| got |
| shot |

But Mr Fox was foxing. What did he do next?

My name is _____

Today is _____

Clues:

Across
1. They went out in a _____.
3. They went up the _____.
4. Dad _____ the boat to a tree.
6. Sally and Dad _____
   and shouted.

1.			2.	

Clues:

Down
2. Dad tied the boat to a _____.
5. The boat was going _____ the river.
7. "Oh no!" said _____.
   "I didn't tie a good knot."

The island picnic   © Nelson Price Milburn. This page is copyright free.

My name is _____

Today is _____

Read and draw. Cut. Read, and write in the numbers. Paste down in the right order.

| 1 | 2 | 3 | 4 |

They all climbed into the boat and went slowly away past the tree-tops.

Sam said, "Look over there." Andy McDonald was coming in his boat to help them.

Sam and Rachel ran to save their toys. Then the muddy, brown water came in.

It had been raining for a week. "The water is coming up fast," said Dad. "The river is in flood."

My name is _____

Today is _____

pl__	fl__		
cr__	br__	fr__	gr__
th__	wh__		

Dad gave Sarah two pet mice.

One was __ __ite. Sarah called it Salt.

The other was __ __own.

Sarah called this one Pepper.

Sarah loved them. She __ __ayed

with them every day, and so did

Nicky __ __om next door.

One day, Nicky took Pepper outside and

put him down on the __ __ass.

Pepper ran into a __ __ower bed.

Nicky went home __ __ying.

Sarah put Pepper's little cage down

by the __ __owers. At bedtime

Sarah looked for Pepper again,

and __ __ere he was sitting

in his old cage. Sarah was __ __eased.

My name is _____

Today is _____

1. Put these words in the right spaces.
   Use some of them twice.

| waved | pushed | helped |
| walked | climbed |

Jessica and Daniel _____ up the hill.

They _____ at Dad. He was at the cow

shed. At the top of the hill Daniel said a

sheep was waving.

It _____ all its legs. Jessica _____ the

fence. They _____ and _____ the sheep

but it was very wet and heavy. Daniel ran to

get Gran. She came up the hill with Daniel

and _____ them push the sheep back onto

its legs.

2. Make new words.

all, ball, _____   like, Mike _____

night, right,  _____   it, sit, _____

wave, save,  _____   ran, Gran, _____

sleep, keep,  _____   let, get, _____

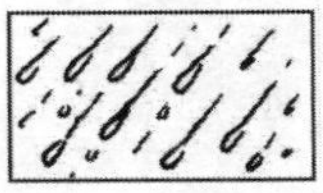

My name is _____

Today is _____

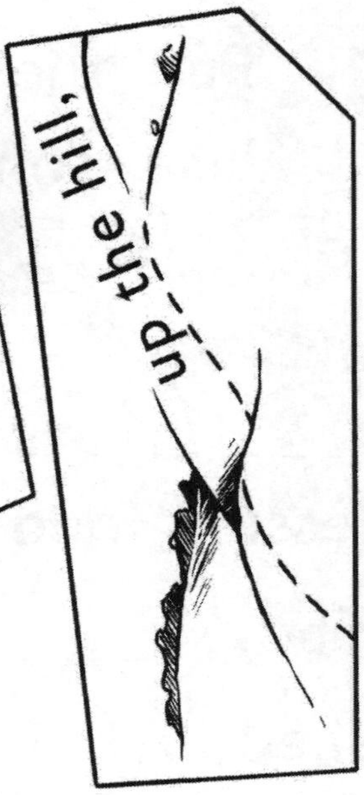

behind the trees,

by the fence,

up the hill,

over the grass,

Past the school,

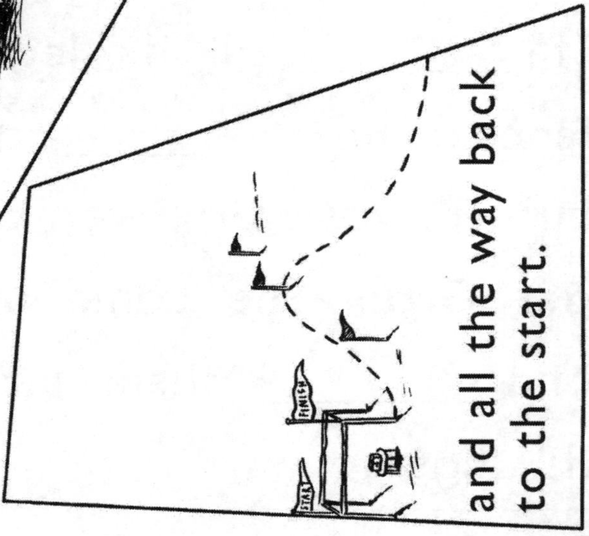

and all the way back to the start.

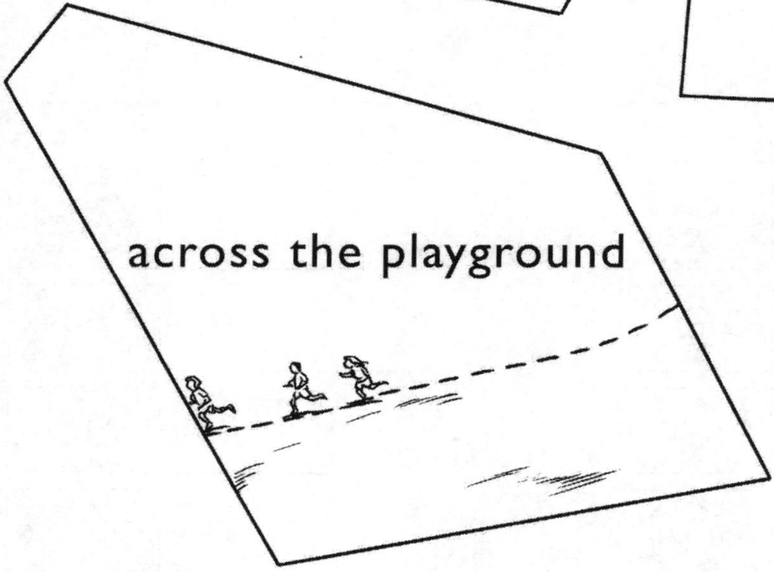

across the playground

round the fort,